A TASTE OF

Gleneagles

A TASTE OF
Gleneagles

David Cranston

Executive Chef

Published by Guinness Books
33 London Road
Enfield
Middlesex EN2 6DJ

Produced and Designed by Mander Gooch Callow

Printed and bound in Italy by
New Interlitho SpA, Milan.

British Library Cataloguing in Publication Data

Cranston, David
A taste of Gleneagles: seasonal recipes
from The Gleneagles Hotel
1. Food. Scottish dishes – Recipes
I. Title
641.59411

ISBN 0-85112-332-5

Photography: Duncan McNicol with art director and stylist Jacquelene Burgess

All photographs were taken at The Gleneagles Hotel in the following locations:
The Strathearn Restaurant; The Conservatory; The Country Club; The Ballroom;
The Glendevon Room; The Dormy House; Braid's Cocktail Bar; The Gleneagles
Jackie Stewart Shooting School Lodge; The Gleneagles Mark Phillips Equestrian Centre;
The loch in the Hotel's grounds; The King's Golf Course.
'Spring' was taken on the banks of the River Tay.

Edited by Martha Lomask and Karen Dolan

CONTENTS

For ease of use many of the basic recipes have been placed as close as possible, where space permits, to the main dishes in which they are used. All the basic recipes are also included in a separate chapter for easy reference.

All spoon measurements are level unless otherwise specified.

Preparation times given are an average calculated during recipe testing.

Metric, Imperial and American measurements have been calculated separately. Use one set of measurements only as they are not exact equivalents.

Cooking times may vary slightly depending on the individual oven.

Always preheat the oven to the specified temperature.

'*At The Gleneagles Hotel we take pride in the quality of the cuisine we offer. We are very fortunate in Scotland to have an abundance of top quality fresh ingredients readily available. At Gleneagles we take full advantage of these, with careful maturing, preparation and finishing, to provide an individual style of cooking and presentation.*

The kitchen is run on the traditional lines first established by Escoffier, while the individual skills of some 55 chefs are nurtured to give The Gleneagles Hotel an elegance of cuisine increasingly rare in today's world.

A Taste of Gleneagles *contains a selection of many of my personal favourites from the Hotel's menus. I hope you will enjoy recreating them for your own guests.* '

David Cranston
Executive Chef at The Gleneagles Hotel

INTRODUCTION

June, 1924. The Morning Post *announced the opening of The Gleneagles Hotel with these words: 'The Scottish Palace in the Glens. The Playground of the Gods.'*

In the years since, The Gleneagles Hotel has proved itself more than worthy of such a glowing description, and has firmly established itself as one of the world's finest hotels. Standing in its own estate, surrounded by the rolling Perthshire hills with the Highlands beyond, the Hotel's situation is unrivalled. It is renowned for its fine cuisine, five-star service, refined and stylish atmosphere and its excellent leisure facilities. The original plans and ambitions of the founders have not only been achieved, but greatly surpassed.

Gleneagles started life as the vision of Donald A. Matheson, a civil engineer and architect, and general manager of the Caledonian Railway Company. Matheson's idea for a luxurious leisure resort came to him while on holiday in Perthshire in 1910. Despite initial opposition, he eventually convinced his company of the enormous potential for success of a development to rival the grand establishments on the Continent of Europe.

Work on the construction of the Hotel, which began in 1913, was interrupted by the First World War, and not resumed until 1922. Building was completed the following year, when the Caledonian Railway Company also amalgamated with the London Midland and Scottish Railway.

The Hotel was fully furbished by 1924, and June of that year saw the suitably lavish gala opening. The Hotel immediately caught the imagination of the public by becoming the first place in the Highlands to host a BBC radio broadcast. The music at the opening ball (conducted by Henry Hall) was heard all over Britain. Thereafter, radio

*programmes were broadcast from the Hotel
twice a week, and Henry Hall's Gleneagles
dance band became a firm favourite with
radio listeners in the 1930s.*

*The British 'travelling class' in the 1920s and
30s were the equivalent of today's jet-setters,
and visitors to Gleneagles in the early days
were the noble, the rich, and the privileged,
who would often arrive at the Hotel's own
railway station with their servants. Many
were attracted by the opportunity to play
golf in beautiful surroundings on first-class
courses.*

*Matheson, whose aim was to create the
perfect resort, wanted golf at Gleneagles to be
the best. To this end, he commissioned a giant
of the golfing world, James Braid, to design
two courses to be laid out in the hotel's
grounds. Braid had won the Open
Championship five times between 1901 and
1910, and with Harry Vardon and J.H. Taylor
formed the famous golfing 'Triumvirate'
which dominated the Open title from 1894,
with 16 victories in 21 years.*

*Braid's two courses at Gleneagles,
named King's and Queen's,
pre-dated the Hotel by a few
years and by 1924 their fame
had spread far and wide.
Golf at Gleneagles was even
advertised in America by
companies such as the White Star
Line, which invited people to
cross the Atlantic in search of the ultimate
golfing experience! Braid himself considered
the Gleneagles courses to be his greatest
achievement; the thirteenth hole on the King's
(the finest, in Braid's opinion), is still called
'Braid's Brawest'.*

*Gleneagles did not only offer excellent golf; it
boasted fine tennis courts, opportunities for
trout fishing in lochs and streams, and
arranged salmon fishing expeditions to the
River Tay. Professionals in their field were on
hand to give lessons (including ballroom*

*dancing) to guests. Gleneagles came to be
known as the 'Mecca of Sport'. It quickly
became* the *place to be seen and newspapers*

and periodicals like The Tatler
*devoted many pages to
the activities of 'Society' in the
luxurious Highland retreat.
Charity balls and galas were
regular events and the
Christmas and New Year
festivities became the highlight
of the social calendar.*

*During the Second World War the Hotel was
taken over by the Ministry of Health for use
as a hospital. It reopened in 1947, and in the
following years went from strength to
strength, expanding and improving its
accommodation and facilities. The growth of
the tourist trade and the increasing
popularity of business conferences meant
that the Hotel began to attract new clients,
thus reaching a wider public.*

*By 1974, when the Hotel held its Golden
Jubilee, 380 guests could be accommodated
in 207 rooms. At the height of the season –
which at that time ran from April to October
– the Hotel employed 400 staff. The Jubilee
was celebrated in true Gleneagles style, with
a banquet and fireworks display, and an
impressive guest list which included the
Russian Ambassador, former Prime Minister
Sir Alec Douglas-Home and other dignitaries.
The toast was proposed by Richard Marsh,
then Chairman of the British Railways
Board. As a fitting finale to the festivities,
Henry Hall led his orchestra in a rendition of
their theme tune: 'Come ye back to bonnie
Scotland'.*

*Today the Hotel is still regarded as one of the
most prestigious in the world. It can now
accommodate a maximum of 450 guests in
240 rooms. Gleneagles' first-class golf courses
have not lost their attraction for golfing
enthusiasts, both professionals and beginners
alike. The King's and Queen's Courses are
regular venues for important competitions.*

In 1986 a long-term commitment was agreed to stage the Bell's Scottish Open Championship on the King's, a venture which is already proving to be a great success. The course is still very much as Braid originally designed it, a testament to its lasting quality.

Although Gleneagles and golf is the first association to spring to mind, the Hotel has far more to offer than its greens and fairways! There are, in fact, few hotels in the world that can match its superb range of sports facilities. It boasts four all-weather tennis courts, a grass court, jogging circuits, pitch and putt, bowling green and croquet lawns.

In addition, the Hotel is home to The Gleneagles Jackie Stewart Shooting School and The Gleneagles Mark Phillips Equestrian Centre. The Shooting School, run by the former Grand Prix champion, teaches many clay target disciplines. The experienced

instructors coach at all levels, enabling novices as well as skilled exponents to enjoy this exhilarating experience. The Equestrian Centre is the most recent development at Gleneagles. Designed and run by Mark Phillips, husband of The Princess Royal and a former Olympic champion, the Centre has been built to exacting world-class standards. It has two heated indoor arenas, an outdoor manège, a stable of handsome horses and many miles of hacking trails. These outstanding facilities, together with the team of horseriding experts, mean that the Centre can cater for all riders, from first-timers to competitors of international standard. There are plans for major equestrian events to be hosted at Gleneagles and televised nationwide. Both the Shooting School and the Equestrian Centre have associated shops which carry specialist clothes and equipment for sale and hire. Over the past few years The Gleneagles Hotel has offered special sporting holiday packages, often hosted by a top name

*in the field, which have proved
extremely popular.*

*The Hotel's facilities were also
extended in 1982 by the addition
of The Country Club, a superb
sporting complex with squash
courts, a fully equipped
gymnasium, billiard and pool
tables, massage and beauty treatments,
saunas and a Turkish bath. The jewel in the
crown is the 22-metre, lagoon-shaped
swimming pool set in a sub-tropical
atmosphere, complete with Jacuzzi and
Canadian hot tubs.*

*The standard of cuisine at The Gleneagles
Hotel has always been acclaimed as nothing
short of splendid, and this reputation for
delicious food persists, playing a major rôle
in earning the Hotel's five red star ranking
with the Automobile Association. The Hotel's
Executive Chef takes full advantage of the
abundance of top quality produce available
in Scotland – beef and lamb, fish and
seafood, game and dairy products. The
Strathearn Restaurant, the Hotel's main
Dining Room, is renowned for its excellence,
offering a Scottish breakfast and exquisite
local game, fish, fresh fruit and vegetables.
The Dormy Grill, which overlooks the 18th
greens of both the King's and Queen's golf
courses, is open from April to October and
features hearty Scottish fare, ideal for
satisfying appetites earned by vigorous
outdoor pursuits. The Country Club brasserie
serves light meals and refreshments by the
poolside, and the Equestrian Centre boasts an
impressive selection of fondues, both savoury
and sweet. The newest restaurant is The
Conservatory, which, true to its name, is sited
in an impressive glass building adjoining
The Strathearn, and whose menu is as
elegant as its setting. 'A Taste of Gleneagles'
offers a seasonal selection of the best dishes
from the Hotel's menus.*

*The Gleneagles Hotel cellars hold 12,000
bottles of wine, ranging from the house claret*

to a magnificent Château Haut Brion! As might be expected in Scotland's top hotel, an extensive selection of whiskies is always available.

There have been three owners of Gleneagles since 1981 – it is now owned by Guinness – but the changes in management have not affected the Hotel's well-being. Each of the successive owners has been dedicated to preserving and enhancing the Hotel's reputation. A stay at The Gleneagles Hotel is a unique and unforgettable experience. It is possible to take a holiday there and never leave the Hotel boundaries. With its own bank and post office, shops, boutiques and hairdresser, Gleneagles is more a self-contained village than a mere hotel! Children and adults alike can enjoy the pleasures of Gleneagles 365 days a year. The elegant hospitality of The Gleneagles Hotel is

legendary and its place as the world's greatest leisure resort unchallenged – truly a dream become reality.

SPRING

Spring symbolises a new beginning, a fresh start,
a time of growth and renewal.

After the excesses of Winter, the early months of
Spring offer the chance to cleanse and
refresh the system, by exercising more and eating
a slightly lighter and healthier diet.

Springtime at Gleneagles means clear, crisp weather,
perfect for brisk walks, invigorating jogs
or a bracing day's fishing on the banks of the Tay.
This season's menus make the most of Spring's
plentiful supply of young vegetables and fresh fish.
Halibut, turbot, trout and sole are all featured,
and that most Scottish of fish, the salmon, appears
smoked, marinated and creamed – in the same recipe!
Fresh vegetables also play a major rôle in
the Chef's Spring collection – broccoli, carrots,
spinach and asparagus, to name
but a few – bringing colour, variety and nutritional
balance to these delicious dishes.

Whether your appetite is the result of vigorous
exercise or energetic spring cleaning,
you will find plenty to satisfy you and your guests
in this season's menu selection.

Salmon fishing on the banks of the River Tay

Marinated Vegetables in Tomato Shells

Sliced Breast of Guinea Fowl with Red Currants

Coconut Tulip

Marinated Vegetables in Tomato Shells

METRIC/IMPERIAL	AMERICAN
6 medium-sized tomatoes	*6 medium-sized tomatoes*
4 cauliflower florets, each approximately 25 g/1 oz	*4 cauliflower florets, each approximately 1 oz*
4 broccoli florets, each approximately 5mm/¼ inch	*4 broccoli florets, each approximately ¼ inch*
12 ears baby corn	*12 ears baby corn*
50 ml/2 fl oz water	*¼ cup water*
1 x 5 ml spoon/1 teaspoon caster sugar	*1 teaspoon superfine sugar*
15 g/½ oz butter	*1 tablespoon butter*
16 button onions	*16 button onions*

Marinade

METRIC/IMPERIAL	AMERICAN
1 egg yolk, size 3	*1 large egg yolk*
40 ml/1½ fl oz malt vinegar	*3 tablespoons cider or white vinegar*
120 ml/4 fl oz walnut oil	*½ cup walnut oil*
salt and pepper	*salt and pepper*
50 g/2 oz crushed cashew nuts	*½ cup crushed cashew nuts*

To garnish

METRIC/IMPERIAL	AMERICAN
about 12 pine-nut kernels	*about 12 pine-nut kernels*
4 sprigs of watercress	*4 sprigs of watercress*

Serves 4

Preparation time: 30 minutes

Cooking time: 20-25 minutes

Marinating time: 4 hours

1 Cut the tomatoes in half horizontally and scoop out the seeds.
2 To make the marinade, place the egg yolk in a bowl, add the vinegar and mix well. Whisk in the oil slowly. Season to taste and add the crushed cashew nuts.
3 Blanch the cauliflower, broccoli and baby corn in salted water for 2 minutes, drain, cool in running cold water and drain again thoroughly. Place the cauliflower and broccoli florets in the marinade and leave to stand for 4 hours. Place the baby corn in a bowl, cover and leave in the refrigerator to use as a garnish.
4 Bring the water and caster sugar to the boil. Add the butter and onions and cook without covering. The water will evaporate during the cooking and the butter will give the onions a nice glaze. Watch them carefully as they cook to avoid burning. Transfer them to a pan and leave to cool.
5 For each serving, fill 3 tomato halves, first with cauliflower, then with broccoli, and top with the button onions. Place them side by side in the centre of a dinner plate and pour a border of the remaining marinade around the tomato halves.
6 Place 3 pieces of baby corn between the tomatoes on each plate, and sprinkle a few pine kernels on top of the sauce. Garnish with a sprig of watercress in the middle.

Sliced Breast of Guinea Fowl with Red Currants

METRIC/IMPERIAL	AMERICAN
4 large wild mushrooms, if available, or freshly-gathered white mushrooms	*4 large fresh mushrooms, if available, or freshly-gathered white mushrooms*
4 oven-ready guinea fowl, boned leaving wings intact, each about 275 g/10 oz	*4 oven-ready guinea fowl, boned leaving wings intact, each about 10 oz*
75 g/3 oz butter	*6 tablespoons butter*
2 shallots, peeled and finely chopped	*2 shallots, peeled and finely chopped*

Marinated Vegetables in Tomato Shells   *Sliced Breast of Guinea Fowl with Red Currants*

1 x 5 ml spoon/1 teaspoon juniper berries, crushed	*1 teaspoon juniper berries, crushed*
200 ml/7 fl oz Veal glaze (page 18)	*¾ cup Veal glaze (page 18)*
salt and pepper	*salt and pepper*
1 x 5 ml spoon/1 teaspoon caster sugar	*1 teaspoon superfine sugar*
100 g/4 oz red currants (fresh or frozen)	*½ cup red currants (fresh or frozen)*

Chicken mousse		
	100 g/4 oz uncooked white chicken meat, skin and bone removed	*4 oz uncooked white chicken meat, skin and bone removed*
	250 ml/8 fl oz double cream	*1 cup heavy cream*
	salt and freshly ground white pepper	*salt and freshly ground white pepper*

To garnish		
	4 x 5 ml spoons/4 teaspoons juniper berries	*4 teaspoons juniper berries*
	4 sprigs rosemary	*4 sprigs rosemary*

Serves 4

Preparation time: 20 minutes

1 To make the chicken mousse, place the chicken meat in a blender or food processor and blend until smooth. Run the purée through a fine sieve. Place in a bowl over ice and add the cream a little at a time, mixing vigorously until a light mousse is produced. Season.

2 Roughly chop the mushrooms and mix them with the chicken mousse.

17

3 Set the guinea fowl on a cutting board, skin side down, and place 2 dessert-spoons (1 rounded tablespoon) of chicken mousse inside each bird. Bring the two ends of the bird together and secure with a wooden cocktail stick (toothpick).
4 Melt half the butter in a heavy-based pan and seal the guinea fowl on all sides. Place in a preheated oven and roast for about 15 minutes.
5 Melt half the remaining butter in a heavy-based pan, add the shallots and lightly sauté, without colouring, for 2 minutes. Mix in the juniper berries and add the veal glaze. Reduce the liquid by a third, season to taste and strain.
6 Melt the remaining butter in a heavy-based pan, add the sugar and stir until dissolved. Add the red currants and 1 dessertspoon (2 teaspoons) of hot water, cover the pan and allow to stew for 2 minutes, without stirring. Remove from the heat.
7 Lay the guinea fowl on a carving board, with the wing bones to the right hand side, and remove the cocktail sticks (toothpicks). At an angle of 45 degrees, carve the bird into 6 even pieces. Place on a plate and gently ease out the slices to form a fan shape.
8 In the hollow of the fan, pour approximately 50 g/2 oz/¼ cup of sauce. Spoon 1 dessertspoon (1 heaped teaspoon) of juniper berrries on top of the sauce and garnish with a sprig of rosemary.

Veal Stock

METRIC/IMPERIAL	AMERICAN
1 kg/2 lb raw veal bones	*2 lb raw veal bones*
225 g/8 oz vegetables	*½ lb vegetables*
(carrots, onions, celery, leeks)	*(carrots, onions, celery, leeks)*
bouquet garni (thyme, bay leaf,	*bouquet garni (thyme, bay leaf,*
parsley stalks)	*parsley stalks)*
6 black peppercorns	*6 black peppercorns*
2 level dessertspoons salt	*4 teaspoons salt*

Makes 1.75 litres/
3 pints/
4 pints (US)

Cooking time:
8-9 hours

Oven: 220°C, 425° F,
Gas Mark 7

1 Chop the bones and brown well on all sides by one of 2 methods: a) place in a roasting tin in a preheated oven for 45 minutes, or b) brown carefully for 10 minutes in a little fat in a frying pan.
2 Drain off any fat and put the bones in a stock pot. Set the roasting tin or frying pan over high heat, and brown the remaining sediment, scraping it from the bottom of the pan with a wooden spoon. Pour in 300 ml/½ pint/1¼ cups of water and simmer for a few minutes, then add to the bones. Do not discard the water. Add 2.25 litres/4 pints/5 pints (US) water. Bring to the boil and skim well.
3 Wash, peel and roughly chop the vegetables and gently fry in a little hot oil or fat until brown. Strain off the fat and add the vegetables to the stock pot. Add the bouquet garni, peppercorns and salt and simmer for 6-8 hours (2 hours for chicken stock). Skim off any froth that rises to the top from time to time. At the end of the cooking time, skim again thoroughly, strain and cool. This stock will keep 3-4 days in a refrigerator, or 2 months if frozen.

Veal Glaze

METRIC/IMPERIAL	AMERICAN
2.25 litres/2 pints Veal stock	*2½ pints Veal stock*
(above)	*(above)*
½ onion, peeled and chopped	*½ onion, peeled and chopped*
6 mushrooms, roughly chopped	*6 mushrooms, roughly chopped*
few parsley stalks	*few parsley stalks*
150 ml/¼ pint dry red wine	*generous ½ cup (5 fl oz) dry red wine*

1 Pour the stock into a heavy-based pan, bring to the boil and reduce to 600 ml/ 1 pint/1¼ pints.
2 Add the onion, mushrooms, parsley and wine and reduce by one-third.

Preparation time: 5 minutes   Cooking time: about 2 hours

Coconut Tulip

	METRIC/IMPERIAL	AMERICAN
Tulip	20 g/¾ oz plain flour	2 level tablespoons all-purpose flour
	40 g/1½ oz ground almonds	4 level tablespoons ground almonds
	100 g/4 oz desiccated coconut	½ cup unsweetened flaked coconut
	1 egg white, size 1	1 jumbo egg white
	15 g/½ oz icing sugar	½ tablespoon confectioners' powdered sugar
Sorbet	200 ml/⅓ pint passion fruit purée (see method)	⅞ cup (7 fl oz) passion fruit purée (see method)
	200 ml/⅓ pint Stock syrup (below)	⅞ cup (7 fl oz) Stock syrup (below)
	200 ml/⅓ pint water	⅞ cup (7 fl oz) water
	1 egg white, size 3, lightly beaten	1 medium egg white, lightly beaten
To finish	Ginger coulis (page 95)	Ginger coulis (page 95)
	175 g/6 oz seasonal berries	1 cup seasonal berries
	mint leaves	mint leaves

Serves 4

Preparation time: 15 minutes

Cooking time: 10-15 minutes

Oven: 110°C, 225°F, Gas Mark ¼

Sorbet making time: 30 minutes

1 To make the tulip, combine all the ingredients and mix until smooth.

2 Lightly grease 2 baking (cookie) sheets. Place 4 teaspoons of the mixture on each sheet, spaced well apart. (The dollops will spread to about 7.5 cm/3 inches in diameter.) Flatten each dollop lightly with the back of a lightly oiled teaspoon.

3 Bake in a preheated oven for 10 – 15 minutes until golden brown. Remove from the oven and leave to cool for a couple of minutes – the rounds must still be pliable. Place each disc over an inverted saucer and lightly press down. Leave to cool for 2-3 minutes – the tulip shapes will be crispy.

4 To make the passion fruit purée, use preserved passion fruit (if available), drained and liquidized, or very ripe fresh passion fruit, peeled and liquidized. To make the sorbet, mix together all the ingredients except the egg white.

5 Pour into an ice-cream or sorbet maker and mix for 15-20 minutes until slushy. (Follow the manufacturer's instructions.) Whisk in the egg white. Pour into a freezer container and store in the deep freeze or freezing compartment of the refrigerator until ready to serve.

6 Place 3 dessertspoons (scant tablespoons) of ginger coulis on each plate. Place the tulip case in the centre and spoon a portion of sorbet into the case. Sprinkle with seasonal berries and decorate with a sprig of mint.

Stock Syrup

	METRIC/IMPERIAL	AMERICAN
	225 g/8 oz caster sugar	1 cup superfine or granulated sugar
	300 ml/½ pint water	1¼ cups water
	juice of 1 lemon	juice of 1 lemon
	juice of 1 orange	juice of 1 orange

Makes 450 ml/ ¾ pint/ scant pint (15 fl oz) (US)

1 Combine all the ingredients in a saucepan and boil until all the sugar has completely dissolved.

2 Strain and leave to cool. Store in a tightly stoppered bottle in the refrigerator.

Preparation time: 20 minutes

Cream of Asparagus Soup with Crushed Toasted Almonds

Trout Mousse Wrapped in Sole with Champagne Cream Sauce

Cinnamon Pastries with Fresh Raspberry Coulis

Cream of Asparagus Soup with Crushed Toasted Almonds

METRIC/IMPERIAL	AMERICAN
50 g/2 oz butter	4 tablespoons butter
50 g/2 oz onion, peeled and chopped	1 small onion (about 2 oz), peeled and chopped
50 g/2 oz flour	scant ½ cup all-purpose flour
1.2 litres/2 pints hot Chicken stock (below)	2½ pints (5 cups) hot Chicken stock (below)
175 g/6 oz asparagus tips, well washed	12 asparagus tips, well washed
salt and pepper	salt and pepper
300 ml/½ pint double cream	1¼ cups heavy cream

To garnish

1 x 5 ml spoon/1 rounded teaspoon chopped chervil	1 rounded teaspoon chopped chervil
50 g/2 oz toasted almonds, crushed	2 level tablespoons toasted almonds, crushed

Serves 4

Preparation time: 15 minutes

Cooking time: 55 minutes

1 Melt the butter in a heavy-based pan and gently cook the onions for about 3-4 minutes, without colouring.
2 Remove from the heat, mix in the flour, then return to low heat and cook, stirring, without colouring, for a few minutes. Remove from the heat and allow to cool slightly.
3 Gradually add the hot stock, mixing well all the time. Return to the heat and stir until simmering point is reached. Add the asparagus tips and salt and pepper and simmer until the asparagus is tender, about 30-40 minutes.
4 Liquidize the soup to a purée and strain through a fine sieve. Add the cream, adjust the seasoning and pour into individual soup bowls. Sprinkle each bowl with chopped chervil and a few toasted almonds.

Chicken Stock

METRIC/IMPERIAL	AMERICAN
1 kg/2 lb raw chicken bones	2 lb raw chicken bones
225 g/8 oz vegetables (carrots, onions, celery, leeks)	½ lb vegetables (carrots, onions, celery, leeks)
bouquet garni (thyme, bay leaf, parsley stalks)	bouquet garni (thyme, bay leaf, parsley stalks)
6 black peppercorns	6 black peppercorns
2 level dessertspoons salt	4 teaspoons salt

Makes 1.75 litres/ 3 pints/ 4 pints (US)

Cooking time: 2-3 hours

1 Chop the bones and brown well on all sides by one of 2 methods: a) place in a roasting tin in a preheated oven for 45 minutes, or b) brown carefully for 10 minutes in a little fat in a frying pan.
2 Drain off any fat and put the bones in a stock pot. Set the roasting tin or frying pan over high heat, and brown the remaining sediment, scraping it from the bottom of the pan with a wooden spoon. Pour in 300 ml/½ pint/1¼ cups of water and simmer for a few minutes, then add to the bones. Do not discard the water. Add 2.25 litres/4 pints/5 pints (US) water. Bring to the boil and skim well.

3 Wash, peel and roughly chop the vegetables and gently fry in a little hot oil or fat until brown. Strain off the fat and add the vegetables to the stock pot. Add the bouquet garni, peppercorns and salt and simmer for 6-8 hours (2 hours for chicken stock). Skim off any froth that rises to the top from time to time. At the end of the cooking time, skim again thoroughly, strain and cool. This stock will keep 3-4 days in a refrigerator, or 2 months if frozen.

Trout Mousse Wrapped in Sole with Champagne Cream Sauce

METRIC/IMPERIAL	AMERICAN
25 g/1 oz butter	*½ tablespoon butter*
4 large sole fillets, skinned	*4 large sole fillets, skinned*
4 large spinach leaves, well washed	*4 large spinach leaves, well washed*
175 g/6 oz sea trout, weighed after skinning and boning	*6 oz sea trout, weighed after skinning and boning*
1 egg white, size 3	*1 medium egg white*
200 ml/⅓ pint double cream	*scant cup (7 fl oz) heavy cream*
salt and pepper	*salt and pepper*
sprigs of dill, to garnish	*sprigs of dill, to garnish*

Champagne sauce

METRIC/IMPERIAL	AMERICAN
25 g/1 oz butter	*½ tablespoon butter*
1 large shallot, peeled and chopped	*1 large shallot, peeled and chopped*
2 sprigs lemon thyme	*2 sprigs lemon thyme*
100 ml/4 fl oz champagne	*½ cup champagne*
200 ml/⅓ pint double cream	*scant cup (7 fl oz) heavy cream*
salt and pepper	*salt and pepper*

Serves 4

Preparation time: 20 minutes, plus chilling

Cooking time: 35 minutes

1 Butter 4 teacups and line each first with a spinach leaf, then with a sole fillet, skinned side inwards.

2 Cut the trout flesh into rough pieces and place in a food processor. Process briefly, then add the egg white and continue to process until the flesh is reduced to a smooth purée. If this is not possible, mince the trout flesh and press through a fine-meshed wire sieve to obtain a purée, then add the egg white.

3 Chill the mixture in a refrigerator for 30 minutes.

4 Set the bowl of purée in a larger bowl of crushed ice. Gradually add the cream, in 8 even stages, then season to taste.

5 Using a piping (pastry) bag fitted with a plain nozzle pipe the mousse into the moulds until level with the top. Wrap each mould in cling film (saran wrap) and steam – either in a wire steaming basket, or on a rack set over simmering water in a large covered saucepan – for about 30 minutes. Test by inserting a small knife blade or skewer; if the mousse is cooked they will come out clean. Remove the mousses from the pan and keep warm.

6 While the moulds are steaming, make the sauce: melt the butter in a pan, add the chopped shallot and thyme and cook, without colouring, for 3-4 minutes. Add the champagne, bring to the boil and reduce rapidly to half the original quantity. Add the cream and reduce by one quarter, until the sauce will coat the back of a spoon. Season and strain.

7 Pour about 75 ml/3 fl oz/a generous ¼ cup of sauce on to each plate. Unwrap the mousses and invert on top of the sauce. Garnish with sprigs of fresh dill.

Cinnamon Pastries with Fresh Raspberry Coulis

	METRIC/IMPERIAL	AMERICAN
Choux pastry	150 ml/¼ pint water	½ cup plus 2 tablespoons water
	pinch of sugar	pinch of superfine or granulated sugar
	50 g/2 oz butter	4 tablespoons butter
	65 g/2½ oz plain flour	½ cup all-purpose flour
	2 eggs, size 1, beaten	2 large eggs, beaten
	vegetable oil, for deep frying	vegetable oil, for deep frying
	15 g/½ oz ground cinnamon	1 tablespoon powdered cinnamon
	40 g/1½ oz caster sugar	3 tablespoons superfine sugar
Filling	250 ml/8 fl oz double cream	1 cup heavy cream
	20 g/¾ oz caster sugar	1½ tablespoons superfine sugar
	2 drops vanilla essence	1 drop vanilla extract
	juice of ½ orange	juice of ½ orange
To serve	175 ml/6 fl oz Raspberry coulis (opposite)	¾ cup Raspberry coulis (opposite)
	4 mint sprigs, to garnish	4 mint sprigs, to garnish

Serves 4

Preparation time: about 20 minutes

Cooking time: 6-8 minutes

1 To make the pastry, bring the water, pinch of sugar and butter to the boil in a heavy-based pan. The butter must be completely melted.

2 Remove from the heat, add the flour all at once and mix vigorously with a wooden spoon until the mixture is smooth and comes away from the sides of the pan. (Do not overbeat – once the paste leaves the sides of the pan, stop.) Leave to cool to lukewarm.

3 Add the beaten eggs a little at a time, stirring constantly until the mixture is of a dropping consistency – if it becomes too thin, the choux puffs will rise unevenly.

4 Place the choux paste in a piping (pastry) bag fitted with a 1 cm/½ inch star nozzle. Pipe small rosettes about 2-2.5 cm/¾-1 inch in diameter on to strips of silicone or waxed paper (5 x 15 cm/2 x 6 inches), to make 16 rosettes.

5 Heat the vegetable oil in a deep fat fryer to 180-190°C/350-375°F, or until a cube of bread browns in 30 seconds. Place a strip of silicone or waxed paper in the hot fat. The pastries will lift off and float – as they do this, carefully remove the paper with tongs. When the pastries are golden brown and puffed (about 5-6 minutes), remove from the fat with a slotted spoon and drain on kitchen paper. Repeat for all the rosettes.

6 Mix the cinnamon and caster (superfine) sugar on a baking (cookie) sheet. Roll the rosettes in the mixture until frosted, then leave to cool.

7 To make the filling, mix the cream, sugar and vanilla in a bowl. Whisk until at piping consistency, then gently stir in the orange juice. Place the mixture in a piping (pastry) bag fitted with a star nozzle.

8 Pierce a hole in the top of each pastry puff and pipe a little cream filling into it.

9 Pour a 'mirror' of raspberry coulis on to each plate and arrange 4 choux puffs on top. Garnish each with a sprig of mint.

Cinnamon Pastries with Raspberry Coulis

Raspberry Coulis

METRIC/IMPERIAL

50 ml/ 2 fl oz water
450 g/1 lb fresh or frozen
raspberries
75 g/3 oz caster sugar

AMERICAN

¼ cup water
1 lb fresh or frozen
raspberries
6 tablespoons (⅜ cup) superfine or
granulated sugar

Makes 300 ml/
½ pint/1¼ cups

Preparation time:
30 minutes

1 Bring the water to the boil in a heavy-based pan, add the raspberries and sugar and simmer until very soft.
2 Press the mixture through a conical strainer, transfer to a jam (jelly) bag and leave suspended over a basin until all the juice has drained through. The bag must be supported so that the bottom of it does not dip into the juice in the basin.
3 Pour the clear juice into a small bowl, cover and refrigerate until ready to serve.

Wholemeal Toasted Croûtons of Smoked, Marinated and Creamed Salmon

	METRIC/IMPERIAL	AMERICAN
	50 g/2 oz boneless salmon	1/8 lb boneless salmon
	salt	salt
	1 x 5 ml spoon/1 teaspoon lemon juice	1 teaspoon lemon juice
	pinch of cayenne pepper	pinch of cayenne pepper
	120 ml/4 fl oz double cream, chilled	¼ cup heavy cream, chilled
	salt and pepper	salt and pepper
	12 toasted wholemeal croûtons (see method)	12 toasted wholewheat croûtons (see method)
	4 thin slices smoked salmon	4 thin slices smoked salmon
	4 thin slices gravadlax	4 thin slices gravlax
Lime sauce	40 ml/1½ fl oz crème fraîche	2 tablespoons crème fraîche or soured cream
	1 x 2.5 ml spoon/½ teaspoon lime juice	½ teaspoon lime juice
	pinch of salt	pinch of salt
	1 x 5 ml spoon/1 teaspoon warm water	1 teaspoon warm water
Saffron sauce	50 g/2 oz mayonnaise	¼ cup mayonnaise
	1 shred saffron, chopped	1 shred saffron, chopped
	salt and pepper	salt and pepper
Mayonnaise **Makes 150 ml** **/5 fl oz/** **½ cup**	1 egg yolk, size 1	1 jumbo egg yolk
	1 x 5 ml spoon/1 teaspoon white wine vinegar	1 teaspoon white wine vinegar
	salt	salt
	ground white pepper	ground white pepper
	a little made mustard	a little made mustard
	120 ml/4 fl oz olive oil	½ cup olive oil
	a little boiling water	a little boiling water
To garnish	1 small carrot, peeled and shredded	1 small carrot, peeled and shredded
	1 small courgette, shredded	1 small zucchini, shredded
	2 radishes, shredded	2 radishes, shredded
	40 g/1½ oz cucumber, shredded	2 tablespoons cucumber, shredded
	25 ml/1 fl oz raspberry vinegar	2 tablespoons raspberry vinegar
	salt and pepper	salt and pepper
	sprigs of dill, parsley and chervil	sprigs of dill, parsley and chervil

Serves 4

Preparation time: 45 minutes

Cooking time:

1 Poach the salmon in salted water for 5 minutes. Remove the skin, put in a food processor or blender and add the lemon juice and cayenne pepper. Blend until smooth and add the double (heavy) cream in 4 even stages, blending briefly between additions. Season to taste.

2 To make the lime sauce, mix the crème fraîche, lime juice and salt and add just enough water to make a thick pouring sauce.

3 To make the saffron sauce, first make the mayonnaise: place the egg yolk, vinegar, seasoning and enough mustard to coat the tip of a knife, in a bowl and whisk well. Gradually pour on the oil, at first drop by drop then as the mayonnaise thickens, in a slow steady stream, whisking continuously. Add the boiling water, whisking well. Divide the mayonnaise between two bowls and stir the saffron into one. Cover the second bowl and refrigerate for another dish.

4 To make the croûtons, cut twelve 4 cm/1½ inch circles from a sliced wholemeal (wholewheat) loaf. Toast on both sides under the grill (broiler).

5 Mix the shredded vegetables together and moisten with the raspberry vinegar. Season to taste.

6 Arrange 3 croûtons in a half moon shape on each plate. On one croûton place a dessertspoon (heaped teaspoon or more) of salmon mousse. Roll a slice of smoked salmon into a cylinder and place on the second croûton. Roll a slice of gravadlax (gravlax) in the same way and place on the third croûton.

7 In front of the croûtons, on one side of the plate, place 2 dessertspoons (heaped teaspoons or more) of saffron sauce and on the other side 2 spoons of the lime sauce.

8 Pile a portion of shredded vegetables into a coffee cup and invert to form a neat mound behind the croûtons. Decorate the salmon croûtons with dill, parsley and chervil respectively.

Fresh Strawberry Sorbet

METRIC/IMPERIAL	AMERICAN
300 ml/½ pint Stock syrup (page 19)	*1¼ cups Stock syrup (page 19)*
75 ml/3 fl oz strawberry purée	*6 tablespoons strawberry purée*
1 egg white, size 3, lightly beaten	*1 medium egg white, lightly beaten*

Serves 4

Preparation time: 8-10 minutes

Freezing time: about 30 minutes

1 Mix together the stock syrup and strawberry purée. Place in a sorbet machine or ice-cream maker and freeze, following the manufacturers' instructions, for about 15 minutes or until slushy.

2 Add the egg white, mix thoroughly and continue to freeze until a sorbet consistency is reached.

3 Place the sorbet in a piping (pastry) bag fitted with a star nozzle and pipe into individual ramekin dishes. Alternatively, scoop the sorbet into a plastic container, cover and place in the freezer. Transfer the sorbet to the refrigerator about 20 minutes before serving.

Rolled Veal and Beef Fillets with Shallots and Garlic

METRIC/IMPERIAL	AMERICAN
4 x 75 g/3 oz pieces veal fillet, cut thin	*4 x 3 oz pieces veal fillet, cut thin*
4 x 75 g/3 oz pieces beef fillet, trimmed into sausage shapes	*4 x 3 oz beef fillet, trimmed into sausage shapes*
25 g/1 oz butter	*2 tablespoons butter*

Sauce

METRIC/IMPERIAL	AMERICAN
150 ml/5 fl oz Beef glaze (page 27)*	*generous ½ cup Beef glaze (page 27)* *
25 g/1 oz butter	*2 tablespoons butter*
1½ cloves garlic, peeled and chopped	*1½ cloves garlic, peeled and chopped*
1 shallot, peeled and chopped	*1 shallot, peeled and chopped*
175 ml/6 fl oz dry red wine	*¾ cup dry red wine*
150 ml/5 fl oz double cream	*generous ½ cup heavy cream*
salt and pepper	*salt and pepper*

To garnish	4 spring onions, blanched and tied in a knot	*4 scallions, blanched and tied in a knot*
	8 pieces carrot, about 2.5 cm/1 inch thick and 5 mm/¼ inch long	*8 pieces carrot, about 1 inch thick and ¼ inch long*
	8 pieces courgette, size as carrots	*8 pieces zucchini, size as carrots*
	4 sprigs of chervil	*4 sprigs of chervil*

*The Beef glaze may be made in advance and stored in a refrigerator until needed.

Serves 4

Preparation time: 30 minutes

Cooking time: 50 minutes

Oven: 230°C, 450°F, Gas Mark 8

1 To make the sauce, first prepare the beef glaze (see below).

2 Melt 25 g/1 oz/2 tablespoons butter and sauté the garlic and shallots, without colouring, for 2-3 minutes. Drain off the butter, add the red wine and bring to the boil. Reduce the liquor by half. Add the beef glaze and simmer for 15 minutes until the sauce coats the back of a spoon. Add the cream and reduce for a further 5 minutes. Season to taste and strain into a jug (pitcher). Keep it warm by standing in a small saucepan of simmering water.

3 Lay the veal fillets on a piece of greaseproof (waxed) paper, cover with another piece of paper and pound flat into thin escalopes. Put a 'sausage' of beef fillet on each escalope of veal and roll, securing with a wooden cocktail stick (toothpick) like a beef olive. Trim off the excess veal to make a neat parcel.

4 Melt the remaining butter in a heavy-based frying pan and seal the meat on all sides. Transfer the veal rolls to a shallow roasting tin and cook in a preheated oven for 5-7 minutes.

5 While the veal is cooking, cook the vegetables: drop the carrots in boiling water and cook for 3 minutes. Add the courgette (zucchini) and cook for one more minute – do not overcook. Drain and refresh under cold running water. Drain and set aside until the meat is almost cooked.

6 Have a steamer ready and reheat the carrots, courgettes (zucchini), and spring onions (scallions).

7 Remove the veal rolls to a warmed platter. Pour 50 ml/2 fl oz/4 tablespoons of sauce on to each of 4 plates. Quickly slice the veal roulades into rings approximately 5 mm/¼ inch thick and place in a cylindrical pattern on top of the sauce. Place the reheated vegetables in the centre and garnish each plate with a sprig of chervil.

Beef Glaze

METRIC/IMPERIAL	AMERICAN
1.2 litres/2 pints Beef stock (page 28)	*2½ pints Beef stock (page 28)*
1 small onion, chopped	*1 small onion, chopped*
2 large mushrooms, washed and roughly chopped	*2 large mushrooms, washed and roughly chopped*
few parsley stalks	*few parsley stalks*
85 ml/3 fl oz dry red wine	*⅓ cup dry red wine*

Makes about 475 ml/ 16-17 fl oz/1 pint (US)

1 Pour the beef stock into a large, heavy-based pan, set over a medium heat and reduce to one-quarter of its original volume: 300ml/½ pint/1¼ cups.

2 Add the chopped onions, mushrooms, parsley and wine and bring to the boil. Reduce the heat to a strong simmer and again reduce the volume by one-third.

In The Strathearn Restaurant: Wholemeal Toasted Croûtons of Smoked, Marinated and Creamed Salmon Rolled Veal and Beef Fillets with Shallots and Garlic

Kiwi Mousse with Mint

METRIC/IMPERIAL	AMERICAN
3 egg yolks, size 2	*3 large egg yolks*
25 g/1 oz caster sugar	*2 level tablespoons superfine sugar*
350 ml/12 fl oz double cream, half-whipped	*1½ cups heavy cream, half-whipped*
2 small kiwi fruit, peeled and puréed	*2 small kiwi fruit, peeled and puréed*
1 large kiwi fruit, peeled and sliced	*1 large kiwi fruit, peeled and sliced*
85 ml/3 fl oz Stock syrup (below)	*6 tablespoons Stock syrup (below)*
few drops mint essence	*few drops essence of peppermint*

Serves 4
Preparation time: 10 minutes

Chilling time: 1 hour

1 Beat the egg yolks and sugar until well blended and fold into the cream.
2 Fold in the kiwi purée lightly, until completely mixed, then divide the mixture between four 15 cm/6 inch goblets or shallow glass bowls. Set a slice of kiwi fruit on top of each mousse.
3 Flavour the cold stock syrup with mint to taste. Spoon about 1½ tablespoons of syrup on top of each mousse. Chill in the refrigerator for 1 hour, then serve immediately.

Stock Syrup

METRIC/IMPERIAL	AMERICAN
225 g/8 oz caster sugar	*1 cup superfine or granulated sugar*
300 ml/½ pint water	*1¼ cups water*
juice of 1 lemon	*juice of 1 lemon*
juice of 1 orange	*juice of 1 orange*

Makes 450 ml/
¾ pint/
scant pint
(15 fl oz) (US)

1 Combine all the ingredients in a saucepan and boil until all the sugar has completely dissolved.
2 Strain and leave to cool. Store in a tightly stoppered bottle in the refrigerator.

Preparation time: 20 minutes

Beef Stock

METRIC/IMPERIAL	AMERICAN
1 kg/2 lb raw beef bones	*2 lb raw beef bones*
225 g/8 oz vegetables	*½ lb vegetables*
(carrots, onions, celery, leeks)	*(carrots, onions, celery, leeks)*
bouquet garni (thyme, bay leaf, parsley stalks)	*bouquet garni (thyme, bay leaf, parsley stalks)*
6 black peppercorns	*6 black peppercorns*
2 level dessertspoons salt	*4 teaspoons salt*

Makes 1.75 litres/
3 pints/
4 pints (US)

Cooking time: 8-9 hours

Oven: 220°C, 425° F, Gas Mark 7

1 Chop the bones and brown well on all sides by one of 2 methods: a) place in a roasting tin in a preheated oven for 45 minutes, or b) brown carefully for 10 minutes in a little fat in a frying pan.
2 Drain off any fat and put the bones in a stock pot. Set the roasting tin or frying pan over high heat, and brown the remaining sediment, scraping it from the bottom of the pan with a wooden spoon. Pour in 300 ml/½ pint/1¼ cups of water and simmer for a few minutes, then add to the bones. Do not discard the water. Add 2.25 litres/4 pints/5 pints (US) water. Bring to the boil and skim well.
3 Wash, peel and roughly chop the vegetables and gently fry in a little hot oil or fat until brown. Strain off the fat and add the vegetables to the stock pot. Add the bouquet garni, peppercorns and salt and simmer for 6-8 hours (2 hours for chicken stock). Skim off any froth that rises to the top from time to time. At the end of the cooking time, skim again thoroughly, strain and cool. This stock will keep 3-4 days in a refrigerator, or 2 months if frozen.

Cucumber Stuffed with Peach and Cheese

METRIC/IMPERIAL	AMERICAN
1 medium cucumber	1 medium cucumber
2 cling peach halves, finely chopped	2 cling peach halves, finely chopped
1 x 5 ml spoon/1 teaspoon chopped chives	1 teaspoon chopped chives
150g/6 oz cottage cheese	¾ cup cottage cheese
assorted salad greens	assorted salad greens
(lollo rosso, frizzy endive,	(chicory, lollo rosso,
lamb's lettuce, etc.)	radicchio, arugula, etc.)
25 ml/1 fl oz shallot vinegar, chilled	1 tablespoon shallot vinegar, chilled
salt and pepper	salt and pepper
1 small red pepper, cored, seeded and cut into very thin strips	1 small red pepper, cored, seeded and cut into very thin strips

Serves 4

Preparation time: 10 minutes

Chilling time: overnight

1 Run a channel cutter down the length of the cucumber about 6 times, making evenly-spaced ridges around the circumference. Cut into quarters and remove the seeds with an apple corer.

2 Place the chopped peaches in a bowl with the chives and cottage cheese and mix thoroughly. Put the mixture in a piping (pastry) bag and fill the hollows of the cucumber pieces. Chill in the refrigerator overnight. Refrigerate any extra peach-cottage cheese mixture, covered with cling film (saran wrap).

3 Place the well-washed salads in a bowl and add the vinegar, salt and pepper. Toss well and put a small mound (about a teacup full) at the top of each plate.

4 Cut 4 thin slices of cucumber, approximately 3 mm/⅛ inch thick, at an angle of 45 degrees and arrange in a fan shape in front of the salad on each plate. Decorate the salad with the pepper strips. Any remaining peach-cottage cheese mixture may be spooned on to each plate if liked.

Rolled Loin of Veal and Lamb with Crushed Hazelnuts and Apricot Sauce

	METRIC/IMPERIAL	AMERICAN
	750 g/1¾ lb boneless veal loin	1¾ lb boneless veal loin
	350 g/12 oz lean, boneless lamb loin	¾ lb lean, boneless lamb loin
	salt and pepper	salt and pepper
	40 g/1½ oz butter	3 tablespoons butter
Mousse	225 g/8 oz boneless chicken breast	½ lb boneless chicken breast
	450 ml/¾ pint double cream	scant 1 pint (15 fl oz) heavy cream
	25 g/1 oz crushed hazelnuts	1 heaped tablespoon crushed hazelnuts
	salt and pepper	salt and pepper
Apricot sauce	300 ml/½ pint Veal glaze (page 30)	1¼ cups Veal glaze (page 30)
	4 dried apricots, cut into thin strips	4 dried apricots, cut into thin strips
	150 ml/¼ pint double cream	½ cup heavy cream
	2 x 5 ml spoons/2 teaspoons chopped parsley	2 teaspoons chopped parsley

Serves 4

**Preparation time:
10 minutes**

**Cooking time:
1 hour 15 minutes**

**Oven: 200°C, 400°F,
Gas Mark 6**

1 Lay the veal loin on its back with the flank open. Lay the lamb on top of the veal and fold over the flank to encase the lamb loin. Roll and secure with string. Season.

2 Melt the butter in a roasting pan and when it is sizzling but not brown, roll the veal to seal on all sides. Roast in a preheated oven for 1¼ hours, basting and turning every 15 minutes.

3 While the veal cooks, make the mousse: finely mince (grind) the chicken and press through a fine sieve into a bowl. Place the bowl over a larger bowl of crushed ice and chill in the refrigerator until very cold. Beat in the cream in several even stages. Mix in the hazelnuts and seasoning. Butter 10 egg-cup-sized moulds, fill with the mousse and cover with cling film (saran wrap). Cook in a steamer (or set on a perforated tray in a wide covered saucepan over simmering water) for 10-12 minutes.

4 While the mousses are steaming, bring the veal glaze to the boil in a small heavy saucepan. Add the dried apricot strips and simmer for about 15 minutes. Add the cream and simmer for a further 15 minutes. Add the chopped parsley.

5 Pour a small amount of sauce on to each plate. Carve the veal and lamb roll into 5 mm/¼ inch slices and serve 2 slices on each plate. Remove the mousses from their moulds and place one on the pool of sauce on each plate.

Veal Glaze

METRIC/IMPERIAL	AMERICAN
2.25 litres/2 pints Veal stock (page 18)	2½ pints Veal stock (page 18)
½ onion, peeled and chopped	½ onion, peeled and chopped
6 mushrooms, roughly chopped	6 mushrooms, roughly chopped
few parsley stalks	few parsley stalks
150 ml/¼ pint dry red wine	generous ½ cup (5 fl oz) dry red wine

**Makes about 475 ml/
16-17 fl oz/1 pint (US)**

1 Pour the stock into a heavy-based pan, bring to the boil and reduce to 600 ml/ 1 pint/1¼ pints.

2 Add the onion, mushrooms, parsley and wine and reduce by one-third.

Preparation time: 5 minutes   Cooking time: about 2 hours

Mango Cheesecake

METRIC/IMPERIAL	AMERICAN
2 egg yolks, size 2, beaten	2 large egg yolks, beaten
40 g/1½ oz caster sugar	3 tablespoons superfine sugar
20 g/¾ oz butter, melted	1½ tablespoons butter, melted
40 g/1½ oz digestive biscuits, crushed	4 tablespoons graham cracker crumbs, medium fine
2 x 5 ml spoons/2 teaspoons lemon juice	2 teaspoons lemon juice
2 x 5 ml spoons/2 level teaspoons powdered gelatine	1 level teaspoon powdered gelatin
175 g/6 oz full fat cream cheese	¾ cup cream cheese
120 ml/4 fl oz mango purée (see method)	½ cup mango purée (see method)
4 large fresh figs (if available), sliced	4 large fresh figs (if available), sliced

**Crystallized
(candied)
lime shreds**

2 limes	2 limes
75g/3 oz caster sugar	6 tablespoons superfine sugar
150 ml/¼ pint water	½ cup (5 fl oz) water

Mango Cheesecake

*Makes 4
individual
cheesecakes*

*Preparation time:
20 minutes*

*Chilling time:
overnight*

1 Beat the egg yolks and sugar together and leave to stand for 10 minutes.

2 Mix together the melted butter and crushed digestive biscuits (graham crackers). Divide the mixture between 4 individual flan rings or tins (tart pans), 7.5 cm/ 3 inches in diameter. Press down well.

3 Prepare the mango purée: use tinned mango slices, drained and liquidized or whirled in a food processor, or very ripe fresh mangoes, peeled, sliced and puréed.

4 Heat the lemon juice in a small pan, add the gelatine and stir to dissolve thoroughly. Mix with the egg and sugar. Place in the bowl of an electric mixer, add the cream cheese and mix at medium speed. As it is mixing, gradually add half of the mango purée. Cover the remaining purée and store in the refrigerator.

5 Pour the cream cheese mixture over the biscuit bases, dividing it evenly between the 4 flan cases. Make sure the tops are level by smoothing with a wetted palette knife (spatula) or the back of a tablespoon. Cover with cling film (saran wrap) and leave to set in the refrigerator overnight.

6 To prepare the crystallized (candied) lime shreds, peel the limes with a vegetable peeler or stripper, making sure that none of the pith clings to the peel. Cut the skin into hair-thin strips of even size.

7 Mix the water and 50 g/2 oz/4 tablespoons of the sugar in a heavy-based pan and bring to the boil. Add the strips of lime peel and boil for a further 5 minutes.

8 Remove the lime peel from the syrup and drain well in a fine sieve. Place the remaining sugar in a jar with a tight lid, add the lime peel, cover and shake vigorously, until all the lime strips are coated with the sugar. Drop the lime shreds into a clean, dry sieve, shake to remove any excess sugar and spread out to dry.

9 To serve, remove the cheesecakes from the flan rings or tins (tart pans). Place one cheesecake in the centre of each plate and pour a little of the reserved mango purée on one side. Arrange the fig slices on the other side. Decorate the top of each cheesecake with a small amount of the crystallized (candied) lime shreds.

31

Sliced Breast of Baby Chicken with Lettuce and Pecan Nut Salad

METRIC/IMPERIAL	AMERICAN
2 roasted baby chickens (poussins), cold	*2 broiler-fryer chickens, about 1 lb each, or 2 Rock Cornish hens, roasted, cold*
4 sprigs chervil, to garnish	*4 sprigs chervil, to garnish*

Dressing

METRIC/IMPERIAL	AMERICAN
1 x 2.5 ml spoon/½ teaspoon English made mustard	*½ teaspoon English mustard*
1 x 5 ml spoon/1 teaspoon white wine vinegar	*1 teaspoon white wine vinegar*
1 egg yolk, size 1	*1 jumbo egg yolk*
2 dessertspoons ground pecan nuts	*2 heaped teaspoons ground pecans*
5 dessertspoons walnut oil	*4 tablespoons walnut oil*
salt and pepper	*salt and pepper*

Salad

METRIC/IMPERIAL	AMERICAN
¼ small green frizzy lettuce	*¼ small green frisée lettuce*
¼ small red frizzy lettuce	*¼ small red frisée lettuce or radicchio*
1 large carrot, grated	*1 large carrot, grated*
4 dessertspoons crushed pecan nuts	*4 heaped teaspoons crushed pecans*

Serves 4

Preparation time: 15 minutes

1 To prepare the dressing, place the mustard, vinegar, egg yolk and ground pecan nuts in a bowl and mix well.

2 Whisk in the walnut oil, a little at a time, until completely incorporated. Season with salt and pepper.

3 Wash and dry the lettuces and divide into small sprigs. Mix with the grated carrot and crushed pecan nuts.

4 Cut the 4 breasts from the chickens and slice each into 5 pieces. For each portion, arrange the 5 slices on a plate in a fan shape. Place a mound of salad at the back of each plate and pour a little dressing next to the salad. Garnish the chicken breasts with a sprig of chervil.

Vegetable Kebab with Wild Rice and Pepper Sauce

METRIC/IMPERIAL	AMERICAN
½ red pepper, cored and seeded	*½ red pepper, cored and seeded*
½ green pepper, cored and seeded	*½ green pepper, cored and seeded*
12 mange-tout pods, topped and tailed	*12 snow pea pods, topped and tailed*
4 radishes	*4 radishes*
4 ears baby corn	*4 ears baby corn*
4 cherry tomatoes	*4 cherry tomatoes*
4 shallots, cooked in salted water	*4 shallots, cooked in salted water*
4 mushrooms	*4 mushrooms*
4 cooked baby beets	*4 cooked baby beets*

Sliced Breast of Baby Chicken with Lettuce and Pecan Nut Salad
Vegetable Kebab with Wild Rice and Pepper Sauce

50 g/2 oz soya, safflower or
sunflower margarine
salt and pepper
175 g/6 oz Wild rice (page 34)

4 tablespoons sunflower,
safflower or soya margarine
salt and pepper
6 oz Wild rice (page 34)

METRIC/IMPERIAL	AMERICAN
25 g/1 oz soya, safflower or sunflower margarine	2 tablespoons sunflower, safflower or soya margarine
½ red pepper, cored, seeded and thinly sliced	½ red pepper, cored, seeded and thinly sliced
½ green pepper, cored, seeded and thinly sliced	½ green pepper, cored, seeded and thinly sliced
½ onion, thinly sliced	½ onion, thinly sliced
1 medium-sized carrot, grated	1 medium-sized carrot, grated
1 x 5 ml spoon/1 teaspoon fresh ginger, finely chopped	1 teaspoon fresh ginger, finely chopped
1 x 5 ml spoon/ 1 teaspoon tomato purée	1 teaspoon tomato purée
300 ml/½ pint vegetable stock	1¼ cups vegetable stock
salt and pepper	salt and pepper
1 heaped 5 ml spoon/1 teaspoon potato starch (fecule)	1 heaped teaspoon potato flour
few drops of soya sauce	few drops of soy sauce
few drops of Worcestershire sauce	few drops of Worcestershire sauce
2 dessertspoons cress heads	small handful watercress leaves

Serves 4

Preparation time: 15 minutes

Cooking time: 35-40 minutes

Oven: 180°C, 350°F, Gas Mark 4

1 Cut 4 round discs out of the red pepper about 2 cm/1 inch in diameter, and 4 identical discs of green pepper.

2 Push 3 pieces of mange-tout (snow peas) to the end of a skewer and open out to form a fan shape.

3 Skewer the remaining vegetables in this order: 1 radish, 1 baby corn, 1 cherry tomato, 1 shallot, 1 piece red pepper, 1 mushroom, 1 piece green pepper, 1 baby beet.

4 Melt the margarine and brush over the kebab. Season with salt and pepper. Place under a hot grill (broiler) for about 1 minute to start the cooking process and to colour the vegetables. Turn over to grill the other side for 1 minute more.

5 Place the kebabs on a rack in a preheated oven and cook for 10 minutes.

6 Cook the Wild rice (see below). Drain and keep warm.

7 To make the sauce, melt the margarine in a heavy-based pan and add the pepper and onion slices. Cook, without colouring, for 1 minute.

8 Add the carrot, ginger and tomato purée and mix well.

9 Add the vegetable stock and salt and pepper and bring to the boil. Reduce the heat and simmer for 10 minutes.

10 Mix the potato starch (potato flour) with a little cold water to make a thin smooth paste, and stir it gradually into the sauce, to thicken. Add the soya (soy) sauce and Worcestershire sauce to taste. Garnish with cress (watercress leaves).

11 Place a little wild rice on a hot dinner plate. Place a kebab diagonally across the plate and gently remove the skewer, taking care not to disturb the vegetables. Pour 3-4 tablespoons of sauce under or over the kebab. Repeat for all servings.

Wild Rice

METRIC/IMPERIAL	AMERICAN
150 g/5 oz wild rice	¾ cup wild rice
600 ml/1 pint water	2½ cups water
15 g/½ oz butter or margarine (optional)	1 tablespoon butter or margarine (optional)
salt and pepper	salt and pepper

Wild rice is not real rice, but a 'water grain', often called 'The Caviar of Grains'. It grows along the margins of lakes in the Northern United States, and traditionally is harvested by hand by local Indian tribes. It is especially delicious with game birds, chicken or turkey or grilled fish.

Serves 4

Preparation time: 5 minutes

1 Wash the wild rice in several changes of cold water. Bring the water and butter (if using) to the boil. Add the rice and seasoning and stir.

2 Cover and simmer gently for about 55 minutes until the rice is tender and all the water is absorbed. Drain thoroughly.

Cooking time: 55 minutes

Flaky Pastry Layered with Pastry Cream and Fondant

METRIC/IMPERIAL	AMERICAN
100 g/4 oz Puff pastry (below)	¼ lb Puff pastry (below)
2 dessertspoons raspberry jam	3 rounded teaspoons raspberry jam
75 g/3 oz Fondant icing	⅜ cup (3 oz) Fondant icing
(page 36)	(page 36)
40 g/1½ oz toasted nibbed almonds	⅓ cup toasted crushed almonds

Pastry cream

METRIC/IMPERIAL	AMERICAN
25 g/1 oz caster sugar	2 tablespoons superfine sugar
25 g/1 oz plain flour	2 tablespoons all-purpose flour
1 egg yolk, size 1	1 large egg yolk
150 ml/¼ pint warm milk	½ cup (5 fl oz) warm milk
zest of ½ orange	zest of ½ orange
zest of ½ lemon	zest of ½ lemon
2 drops vanilla essence	2 drops vanilla extract

Serves 4

Preparation time: 25 minutes

Cooking time: 15-20 minutes

Oven: 120°C, 225°F, Gas Mark ½

1 Roll out the pastry to form a rectangle 15 x 20 cm (6 x 8 inches), 3mm/⅛ inch thick. Prick several times all over with a fork.

2 Wrap the pastry in cling film (saran wrap) and chill for 20 minutes.

3 Cut the pastry into 3 rectangular pieces, each 7.5 x 10 cm/3 x 4 inches. Place on a wetted baking (cookie) sheet and bake in a preheated oven for 15-20 minutes. Set aside to cool on a rack.

4 Meanwhile, make the pastry cream: mix the sugar, flour and egg yolks in a bowl.

5 Infuse the zest of orange and lemon in warm milk for 5 minutes. Bring the milk to the boil and add the vanilla essence (extract).

6 Pour the milk on to the sugar, flour and egg mixture, whisking constantly. Return the mixture to a clean pan and bring to the boil, whisking all the time. When the mixture has boiled, pour into a bowl and leave to cool.

7 On one piece of pastry spread a layer of raspberry jam followed by a layer of pastry cream 5 mm/¼ inch thick. Place a second piece of pastry on top and spread it with jam and pastry cream. Place the remaining piece of pastry on top of this.

8 Warm the fondant over a pan of hot water to make it pliable and almost liquid. Pour carefully over the top of the pastry.

9 With a warm, wet palette knife (spatula) spread the fondant evenly over the top surface; do not worry about about any that runs over the edge. Again using a palette knife (spatula), smooth off the edges of the pastry and decorate the sides with the toasted nibbed (crushed) almonds. Cut the pastry into 4 even-sized pieces with a sharp knife.

Puff Pastry

METRIC/IMPERIAL	AMERICAN
225 g/8 oz plain flour	½ lb (1½ cups) all-purpose flour
salt	salt
225 g/8 oz margarine or butter, very cold	½ lb margarine or butter, very cold
150 ml/¼ pint ice-cold water	generous ½ cup (5 fl oz) ice-cold water
few drops of lemon juice	few drops of lemon juice

Note: care must be taken when rolling out the paste to keep the ends and sides square. The lightness of the paste is caused by the air which is trapped when folding the pastry during preparation.

*Makes 500 g/
1¼ lb*

*Preparation time:
20 minutes*

*Resting time:
1 hour 50 minutes*

1 Sift the flour and salt into a bowl. Rub or cut in with a pastry blender, 50 g/2 oz/ 4 tablespoons of the fat.

2 Make a well in the centre and add the water and lemon juice. Knead well into a smooth dough to form a ball. Leave the dough to rest in a cool place for 30 minutes.

3 Cut a cross half way through the dough and pull out the corners to form a star shape. Roll out the points of the star square, leaving the centre thick.

4 Knead the remaining fat to the same texture as the dough. (This is most important: if the fat is too soft it will melt and ooze out, if too hard it will break through the paste when being rolled.)

5 Place the fat on the thick centre of the star shape and fold over the flaps. Roll out to approximately 30 x 15 cm/12 x 6 inches, cover with a cloth and leave to rest in a cool place for 20 minutes.

6 Roll out to approximately 60 x 20 cm/24 x 8 inches, fold both ends into the centre and fold in half again to form a square – this is one double turn. Leave to rest in a cool place for 20 minutes.

7 Half turn the paste to the right or left and roll out again. Give one more double turn (Step 6), roll out and leave to rest for 20 minutes. Give the pastry 2 more double turns, rolling out and resting between each turn. Leave to rest for another 20 minutes before using.

Fondant Icing

METRIC/IMPERIAL	AMERICAN
225 g/8 oz granulated sugar	*½ lb superfine or granulated sugar*
120 ml/4 fl oz water	*½ cup water*
½ teaspoon liquid glucose or pinch of cream of tartar	*pinch of cream of tartar*

*Makes 225 g/
8 oz/½ lb*

*Preparation time:
about 15 minutes*

*Cooking time:
10-15 minutes*

1 In a small deep saucepan, stir the sugar into the water over a low heat. Do not allow it to boil.

2 In a saucer, stir the cream of tartar to a smooth consistency with about a teaspoonful of water. Add to the sugar syrup. Cover and bring to the boil – when you hear it begin to simmer remove the cover. Insert a sugar or deep- frying thermometer and boil the mixture to 115°C/240°F. If you do not have a thermometer, cook until a small spoonful dropped into a bowl of ice-cold water will form a soft ball when kneaded between the fingers. Remove from the heat and stand the pan in a deeper pan of cold water to cool slightly.

3 Run cold water over a cold smooth surface (ideally, marble). Pour on the fondant and with a palette knife (spatula), turn the outside edges towards the centre. Keep on turning it in on itself until it is moderately stiff, and begins to look grainy and opaque. Scrape it up into a ball and knead it with your hands until it is smooth and even.

4 To use within a few hours: place the fondant ball in a bowl and cover with a damp cloth.

5 To store: place in an airtight tin or a jar with a tight screw top. Before use, warm it in a bowl over hot water.

6 Fondant can be rolled out on a board covered lightly with icing (confectioners' powdered) sugar and cut into the desired shape.

Vegetable Gâteau with Tomato and Basil Purée

METRIC/IMPERIAL	AMERICAN
assorted salad greens (e.g. lollo rosso, frizzy endive, radicchio, lamb's lettuce)	assorted salad greens (e.g chicory, radicchio, red-edged lettuce, arugula)
100 ml/4 fl oz port	½ cup port
100 ml/4 fl oz vegetable stock (made from cube)	½ cup vegetable stock (made from cube)
4 x 5 ml spoons/4 teaspoons powdered gelatine	4 teaspoons gelatin powder
few thyme leaves	few thyme leaves
200 g/7 oz cooked carrot purée	1 cup cooked carrot purée
200 g/7 oz cooked broccoli purée	1 cup cooked broccoli purée
1 tablespoon liquid honey	1 tablespoon liquid honey
450 ml/¾ pint	scant pint (15 fl oz)
double cream	heavy cream
2 sprigs thyme	2 sprigs thyme
salt and pepper	salt and pepper
Tomato coulis (page 38)	Tomato coulis (page 38)
4 basil leaves, to garnish	4 basil leaves, to garnish

Serves 4

Preparation time: 30 minutes, plus chilling

Cooking time: 15 minutes

1 Wash, dry and chill the salad greens.

2 Pour the port and the vegetable stock into a pan and heat gently. Add 1 x 5 ml spoon/1 teaspoon of gelatine and allow to dissolve.

3 Sprinkle a few pieces of thyme leaf in the bottom of 4 individual ramekin dishes. Pour the port aspic (the gelatine mixture) over the leaves to a depth of about 3 mm/⅛ inch and leave to set.

4 Place the cold puréed carrots and cold puréed broccoli into 2 separate pans. Add half the honey and half the cream to each pan and bring to simmering point. Add 2 x 5 ml spoons/2 teaspoons of gelatine to each pan and remove from the heat when dissolved. Season to taste.

5 Divide the carrot mousse between the ramekins (they should be no more than half full). Chill in the refrigerator for 30 minutes.

6 Carefully pour the broccoli mousse on top, filling the ramekin dishes to the top. Chill in the refrigerator until set.

7 Meanwhile, prepare the tomato coulis (page 38).

8 Fill a teacup with salad and invert on to a plate to form a neat mound. Repeat for the other 3 portions. Loosen each vegetable gâteau from the mould with a sharp-pointed knife and turn upside down in the centre of each plate.

9 Coat half of each gâteau with the tomato coulis and garnish with a basil leaf.

Vegetable Gâteau with Tomato and Basil Purée　　　*Broiled Halibut and Turbot Steaks with Sauces of Rosemary and Sorrel*

Tomato Coulis

METRIC/IMPERIAL	AMERICAN
25 g/1 oz butter	*2 tablespoons butter*
¼ medium onion, chopped	*1 small onion, chopped*
3 basil leaves, chopped	*3 basil leaves, chopped*
10 tomatoes, roughly chopped	*10 tomatoes, roughly chopped*
few drops of Tabasco	*few drops of Tabasco*
1 x 2.5 ml spoon/½ teaspoon Worcestershire sauce	*½ teaspoon Worcestershire sauce*
salt and pepper	*salt and pepper*

Makes 600 ml/ 1 pint/1¼ pints (US)

1 Melt the butter in a pan, add the onion and chopped basil and cook gently for a few minutes.
2 Add the tomatoes, cover the pan and cook for about 15 minutes until very soft.
3 Pour the mixture into a liquidizer, add the sauces and blend well. Season.
4 Strain the sauce through a fine sieve to remove all skin and seeds. Leave to cool.

Broiled Halibut and Turbot Steaks with Sauces of Rosemary and Sorrel

	METRIC/IMPERIAL	AMERICAN
Sauce	15 g/½ oz butter	1 tablespoon butter
	25 g/1 oz shallots, peeled and chopped	2 tablespoons shallots, peeled and chopped
	50 ml/2 fl oz dry white wine	¼ cup dry white wine
	250 ml/8 fl oz Fish stock (below)	1 cup Fish stock (below)
	450 ml/¾ pint double cream	scant pint (15 fl oz) heavy cream
	1 x 5 ml spoon/1 level teaspoon rosemary, chopped	1 level teaspoon rosemary, chopped
	1 x 5 ml spoon/1 level teaspoon sorrel, chopped	1 level teaspoon sorrel, chopped
	2 halibut steaks, about 1 cm/½ inch thick (900g/2 lb total weight)	2 halibut steaks, about ½ inch thick (2 lb total weight)
	2 turbot steaks, about 1 cm/½ inch thick (900 g/2 lb total weight)	2 turbot steaks, about ½ inch thick (2 lb total weight)
	100 g/4 oz butter	½ cup butter
	salt and pepper	salt and pepper
	plain flour, for dusting	all-purpose flour, for dusting
To garnish	1 small ripe tomato, peeled, seeded and cut into 5 mm/¼ inch dice	1 small ripe tomato, peeled, seeded and cut into ¼ inch dice

Serves 4

Preparation time: 30 minutes

Cooking time: 45 minutes

1 To make the sauce: melt the butter in a heavy-based pan and fry the shallots for about 2 minutes, without colouring. Add the wine, bring to the boil and reduce by half. Add the stock, bring to the boil and reduce by half.
2 While the sauce is reducing, cut each fish steak in half so that you have eight 'steaklets'. Dot with butter, season and dust with flour. Grill (broil) under medium heat until cooked but not coloured.
3 Add the cream to the sauce and reduce by a quarter until of coating consistency.
4 Divide the sauce between two warmed bowls: stir the chopped rosemary into one and the chopped sorrel into the other.
5 Arrange the cooked steaklets alternately, in a half-moon shape on each plate. Coat one side of the plate with rosemary sauce, the other with sorrel sauce. Put the diced tomato in the centre. Serve with Wild rice and Pommes rosti (page 40).

Fish Stock

	METRIC/IMPERIAL	AMERICAN
	25 g/1 oz butter or margarine	2 tablespoons butter or margarine
	100 g/4 oz onions, peeled and sliced	1 medium onion, peeled and sliced
	1 kg/2 lb white fish bones (preferably sole, whiting, turbot, etc), viscera and gills removed	2 lb white fish bones from any non-oily fish (flounder, sole, whiting, weakfish), viscera and gills removed
	1 bay leaf	1 bay leaf
	juice of ½ small lemon	juice of ½ a small lemon
	parsley stalks	parsley stalks
	3 peppercorns	3 peppercorns
	2.25 litres/4 pints water	5 pints water

Makes 1.75 litres/ 3 pints/3¾ pints (US)

Preparation time: 10 minutes

Cooking time: 30 minutes

1 Melt the butter or margarine in a very large heavy-based pan. Add the onions, fish bones and all the other ingredients except the water. Cover the pan with greaseproof (waxed) paper and a lid and cook gently for 5 minutes.
2 Remove the paper and add the water. Bring to the boil, skim and simmer for 20 minutes only. Strain and cool.
3 Chill in the refrigerator, where it will keep for 2-3 days. Fish stock can be frozen for up to 1 month.

Wild Rice

METRIC/IMPERIAL	AMERICAN
150 g/5 oz wild rice	¾ cup wild rice
600 ml/1 pint water	2½ cups water
15 g/½ oz butter or	1 tablespoon butter or
margarine (optional)	margarine (optional)
salt and pepper	salt and pepper

Wild rice is not real rice, but a 'water grain', often called 'The Caviar of Grains'. It grows along the margins of lakes in the Northern United States, and traditionally is harvested by hand by local Indian tribes. It is especially delicious with game birds, chicken or turkey or grilled fish.

Serves 4

Preparation time: 5 minutes

Cooking time: 55 minutes

1 Wash the wild rice in several changes of cold water. Bring the water and butter (if using) to the boil. Add the rice and seasoning and stir.
2 Cover and simmer gently for about 55 minutes until the rice is tender and all the water is absorbed. Drain thoroughly.

Pommes Rosti

METRIC/IMPERIAL	AMERICAN
4 large potatoes	4 large potatoes
salt and pepper	salt and pepper
20 g/¾ oz butter	scant 2 tablespoons butter
40 ml/1½ fl oz (3 tablespoons)	3 tablespoons cooking oil
cooking oil	

Serves 4

Preparation time: 5 minutes

Cooking time: about 35 minutes

Oven: 200°C, 400°F, Gas Mark 6

1 Wash and peel the potatoes and coarsely grate into a bowl. Press hard through a sieve, then wring out in a dry tea towel, to remove excess moisture. (Wash the towel immediately as the potato juice will stain.) Season with salt and pepper.
2 Melt the butter with the oil in an ovenproof frying pan and heat until the mixture starts to smoke. Pour the grated potatoes into the pan, emptying the bowl away from you, to avoid being splashed with hot oil.
3 Press the mixture down with a palette knife (wide spatula), to ensure an even thickness across the pan. The mixture should resemble a thick pancake. Cook until the underside forms a golden-brown crust.
4 Using a palette knife or fish slice (pancake turner), carefully remove the rosti from the pan. (Alternatively, place an inverted plate over the pan and slide the potatoes out). Add a little more oil to the pan and heat until hot, tilting the pan to coat the bottom and sides of the pan thoroughly. Return the potato mixture to the pan, cooked-side up.)
5 Place in a preheated oven and cook for about 15 minutes until the potatoes are cooked through.
6 Turn the rosti out on to a baking tin or plate and leave to cool slightly. Cut into 4 rounds, using a 7.5 cm/3 inch diameter cutter.

Pear and Frangipane Tart with Butterscotch Sauce

METRIC/IMPERIAL	AMERICAN
175 g/6 oz (¾ recipe) Sweet pastry (below)	6 oz (¾ recipe) Sweet pastry (below)
50 g/2 oz butter	¼ cup butter
50 g/2 oz caster sugar	4 tablespoons superfine sugar
1 egg, size 1, beaten	1 jumbo egg, beaten
50 g/2 oz ground almonds	⅔ cup ground almonds
10 g/¼ oz (1 level tablespoon) plain flour	1 level tablespoon all-purpose flour
1 medium pear, or 2 small, peeled and cut into 5 mm/¼ inch dice	1 medium pear or 2 small, peeled and cut into ¼ inch dice

	METRIC/IMPERIAL	AMERICAN
Sauce	40 g/1½ oz Demerara sugar	3 level tablespoons light brown sugar
	40 g/1½ oz butter	3 level tablespoons butter
	150 ml/¼ pint double cream	generous ½ cup (5 fl oz) heavy cream

Makes 4 individual tarts

Preparation time: 20 minutes

Cooking time: 50 minutes – 1 hour

Oven: 120°C, 250°F, Gas Mark ½
then: 150°C, 300°F, Gas Mark 2

1 Line 4 individual tart tins, 10 cm/4 inches diameter and 2 cm/¾ inch deep, with sweet pastry. Prick the bases with the tines of a fork and bake blind in a preheated oven for 3-4 minutes. Remove and leave to cool slightly.

2 While the pastry is baking, make the filling : beat the butter and sugar together until light and fluffy. Beat in the egg, then lightly fold in the almonds, flour and diced pears.

3 Fill the pastry cases with the mixture, reduce the oven temperature and bake for 25-30 minutes.

4 Meanwhile, make the sauce: mix all the ingredients in a heavy-based pan and bring to the boil. Lower the heat and simmer for 10 minutes. Remove from the heat and leave to cool.

5 Gently slide the tarts out of the tins on to a rack and cool. Pour a pool of butterscotch sauce on each plate and set a tart on top. Serve at once.

Sweet Pastry

METRIC/IMPERIAL	AMERICAN
65 g/2½ oz butter	2 oz plus 2 tablespoons butter
25 g/1 oz caster sugar	2 tablespoons superfine sugar
½ egg, size 4, beaten	1 very small egg, beaten
100 g/4 oz flour	1 cup all-purpose flour

Makes 225 g/8 oz

1 Cream together the butter and sugar.
2 Add the egg gradually, then mix in the flour to form a dough.
3 Chill for 30 minutes before rolling out.

SUMMER

Summer is the season of 'lazy, hazy days',
ideal for picnics, leisurely strolls and all manner
of outdoor pursuits. At Gleneagles these
include tennis, swimming, bowls, croquet and cycling.

Summer food is traditionally light, refreshing
and bursting with goodness. It is a time
for crisp salads, fresh herbs, succulent strawberries
and cool ice-creams. Summer menus benefit
from the abundance of delicious fresh ingredients
available at this time of year.

This season the Chef presents a variety of delectable
dishes, perfect for warm, sultry weather – cold starters
and chilled desserts, fresh seafood, healthy
salads, mouthwatering meringues and juicy berry fruits.

These menus will enhance any Summertime occasion,
whether taking afternoon tea on
the veranda or dining in the evening 'al fresco'.

Cream Cheese with Parma Ham (Prosciutto)

METRIC/IMPERIAL	AMERICAN
12 paper-thin slices Parma ham (prosciutto), each approximately 15 x 5 cm/6 x 4 inches	12 paper-thin slices prosciutto, each approximately 6 x 4 inches
100 g/4 oz cream cheese	¼ lb cream cheese
assorted lettuces (lollo rosso, lamb's lettuce, etc)	assorted lettuces (endive, radicchio, arugula)
1½ dessertspoons balsamic vinegar	1½ teaspoons balsamic vinegar
4 spring onions	4 scallions
4 radishes	4 radishes
4 cherry tomatoes	4 cherry tomatoes
8 baby corn cobs	8 baby corn cobs
12 chives	12 chives

Serves 4

Preparation time: 10 minutes

Cooking time: about 2 minutes

Oven: 140°C, 275°F, Gas Mark 1

1 Lay out the slices of Parma ham (prosciutto) and spoon 25 g /1 oz of cream cheese in the centre of each slice.

2 Roll up the slices and shape into parcels of approximately 2 x 2.5 cm/¾ x½ inch.

3 Place the parcels on a baking (cookie) sheet and cook in a preheated oven for 1-2 minutes, until the cheese inside has melted slightly.

4 Wash and dry the lettuces and place in a bowl. Add the vinegar and toss to mix.

5 Place a mound of salad on each plate. Arrange 3 ham and cheese parcels in a curve. At the back of each plate, arrange the spring onion (scallions), radish, cherry tomato and 2 baby corn cobs. Garnish each with 3 chives.

Smoked Mackerel, Baby Herring and Mussel Salad with Mustard and Caviar Dressing

METRIC/IMPERIAL	AMERICAN
24 smoked mussels	24 smoked mussels
juice of 1 lime	juice of 1 lime
½ dessertspoon malt vinegar	1 teaspoon cider vinegar
½ dessertspoon olive oil	1 teaspoon olive oil
2 dessertspoons chopped chives	2 rounded teaspoons chopped chives
1 dessertspoon chopped shallot	1 rounded teaspoon chopped shallot
2 smoked mackerel fillets, skinned and boned	2 smoked mackerel fillets, skinned and boned
4 smoked baby herring fillets, skinned and boned	2 smoked baby herring fillets, skinned and boned
1 bunch mustard and cress	1 bunch watercress, leaves only
8 dessertspoons crème fraîche or soured cream	4 tablespoons crème fraîche or sour cream
4 sprigs chopped dill	4 sprigs chopped dill
2 dessertspoons dry white wine	3 teaspoons dry white wine
1 dessertspoon Scottish wholegrain mustard	1 rounded teaspoon wholegrain mustard
salt and pepper	salt and pepper
25 g/1 oz Keta (red) caviar	1 oz red salmon caviar

Serves 4

Preparation time:
20 minutes

Marinating time:
2 hours

1 Place the mussels in a bowl with the lime juice, vinegar, olive oil, chives and shallot and leave to marinate for 2 hours.

2 For each serving, place 6 mussels in an empty scallop shell and set in the centre of a dinner plate.

3 Scallop each mackerel fillet into 6 pieces and, using 3 pieces per portion, arrange on the dinner plate to one side of the shell. Scallop the herring fillet into 6 pieces and, again using 3 pieces per serving, place on the dinner plate to the other side of the shell. Tuck some well-washed mustard and cress (watercress leaves) into the back of each scallop shell.

4 To make the sauce, mix the crème fraîche (or soured cream) with the dill, wine and mustard. Taste and adjust the seasoning.

5 Pour 2 dessertspoonfuls/2 heaped teaspoons of sauce on to the plate in front of the scallop shell and sprinkle the Keta (red salmon) caviar over the sauce.

By the pool in The Country Club: Cream Cheese with Parma Ham (Prosciutto)
Smoked Mackerel, Baby Herring and Mussel Salad with Mustard and Caviar Dressing

Milk, Plain and White Chocolate Mousses

AMERICAN

20 g/¾ oz milk chocolate
20 g/¾ oz plain chocolate
20 g/¾ oz white chocolate
300 ml/½ pint double cream
20 g/¾ oz caster sugar

1 square milk chocolate
1 square bitter chocolate
1 square white chocolate
1¼ cups heavy cream
1½ tablespoons superfine or
granulated sugar

Sauce 300 ml/½ pint milk
zest of 1 orange
3 egg yolks, size 2, beaten
25 g/1 oz caster sugar
2 drops vanilla essence
25 ml/1 fl oz dark rum

1¼ cups milk
zest of 1 orange
3 jumbo egg yolks, beaten
2 tablespoons superfine sugar
2 drops vanilla extract
2 tablespoons dark rum

To decorate sprigs of fresh mint
chocolate shavings

sprigs of fresh mint
chocolate shavings

Use top quality cooking (couverture) chocolate of all three kinds, obtainable from good grocers and gourmet food shops. If unobtainable, use best quality eating chocolate.

Serves 4

Preparation time: 10 minutes

Chilling time: overnight

Cooking time: 10-15 minutes

1 Melt each of the 3 chocolates in a separate glass bowl over hot water without stirring, and without allowing steam or hot water to touch the chocolate.

2 Half-whip the cream with the sugar and divide into 3 bowls. Gently mix the melted chocolates separately into the portions of whipped cream so that you have a bowl of milk chocolate mousse, a bowl of plain dark chocolate and a bowl of white chocolate. Cool completely, cover with cling film (saran wrap) and refrigerate overnight.

3 To make the sauce, heat the milk and the orange zest to simmering point.

4 Meanwhile, mix the egg yolks, sugar and vanilla essence (extract) in a bowl until light and fluffy.

5 Add this mixture to the hot milk, mix well and pour into a heavy-based pan. Place over a low heat and, stirring constantly with a wooden spoon, bring back to simmering point, until the mixture coats the back of the spoon. Do not boil – the mixture will instantly curdle.

6 Strain the mixture into a bowl and leave to cool. Mix in the rum.

7 To serve, take 1 dessertspoonful of each of the 3 mousses and arrange on a chilled plate. Pour a border of sauce around the mousses and decorate with mint sprigs and chocolate shavings. Repeat for each serving.

Watercress Soup with Fresh Thyme and Cream

METRIC/IMPERIAL

AMERICAN

40 g/1½ oz butter	*2½ tablespoons butter*
1 medium onion, peeled and finely chopped	*1 medium onion, peeled and finely chopped*
1 large stick celery, trimmed and finely chopped	*1 large stick celery, trimmed and finely chopped*
1 leek, well washed and finely chopped	*1 leek, well washed and finely chopped*
1 x 2.5 ml spoon/½ teaspoon chopped fresh thyme	*½ teaspoon chopped fresh thyme*
1 large or 2 small bunches watercress (leaves only), roughly chopped, a few leaves reserved for garnish	*1 large or 2 small bunches watercress (leaves only), roughly chopped, a few leaves reserved for garnish*
1 litre/1¾ pints Chicken stock (page 51)	*2¼ pints Chicken stock (page 51)*
225 g/8 oz potatoes, peeled and roughly chopped	*½ lb potatoes, peeled and roughly chopped*
65 ml/2½ fl oz double cream	*¼ cup heavy cream*
salt and pepper	*salt and pepper*

Serves 4

Preparation time: 15 minutes

Cooking time: 1 hour 10 minutes

1 Melt the butter in a heavy-based pan and add the onion, celery, leek and thyme. Cook for a couple of minutes, without colouring.

2 Add the chopped watercress and cook for a further 5 minutes, without colouring, then add the chicken stock and potatoes. Bring to the boil, then simmer for approximately 1 hour or until all the ingredients are cooked thoroughly.

3 Liquidize the soup, then strain through a fine strainer into a clean bowl. Add the cream and adjust the seasoning. Reheat gently if necessary.

4 Pour into individual bowls and garnish with the reserved watercress leaves.

Escalope of Veal with Braised Chinese Cabbage

METRIC/IMPERIAL

AMERICAN

25 g/1 oz butter	*2 tablespoons butter*
1 onion, thinly sliced	*1 onion, thinly sliced*
4 rashers streaky bacon, shredded	*4 strips bacon, shredded*
1 medium-sized head Chinese cabbage, shredded	*1 medium-sized head Bok Choy, shredded*
pinch of nutmeg	*pinch of nutmeg*
salt and pepper	*salt and pepper*
4 x 200 g/7 oz veal escalopes, trimmed	*4 x 7 oz veal escalopes, trimmed*
50 g/2 oz Clarified butter (page 48)	*4 tablespoons Clarified butter (page 48)*
1 shallot, finely chopped	*1 shallot, finely chopped*
50 ml/2 fl oz brandy	*4 tablespoons brandy*
300 ml/½ pint double cream	*1¼ cups heavy cream*
75 g/3 oz Gruyère cheese, grated	*¾ cup Swiss cheese, grated*
2 dessertspoons chopped chives, to garnish	*2 level tablespoons chopped chives, to garnish*

47

Serves 4

Preparation time:
15 minutes

Cooking time:
about 20 minutes

Oven: 200°C, 400°F,
Gas Mark 6

1 Melt 25 g/1 oz/2 tablespoons butter in a pan, add the onion and cook, without colouring, for 2-3 minutes.
2 Add the bacon, cabbage (Bok Choy), nutmeg and seasoning. Cook over a high heat for about 3-4 minutes, stirring constantly. Strain off the excess juice. Cool.
3 Lay each escalope flat on a chopping board and sprinkle with salt and pepper. Place a dessertspoonful/level tablespoon of cabbage mixture on one half of the escalope, fold in half so that the edges meet and lightly pinch the edges together.
4 Melt the clarified butter in an ovenproof pan and fry the escalopes until the undersides only are coloured. Turn over and place in a preheated oven for 10-12 minutes. Transfer to an ovenproof shallow serving dish and keep warm.
5 Drain off all but about 1 tablespoon of the excess juices from the pan. Add the shallots and cook, without colouring, for 30 seconds.
6 Add the brandy and reduce the liquid by half. Add the cream, bring to the boil and simmer until reduced by half again. Adjust the seasoning.
7 Heat the grill (broiler). Strain the sauce over the escalopes, making sure they are completely covered. Sprinkle the top of each escalope with the grated Gruyère (Swiss) cheese and place under the grill (broiler) until the cheese has melted. Garnish with chopped chives.

Clarified Butter

Makes 500 g/1¼ lb/
20 oz

1 Melt 1 kg/2 lb/32 oz salted butter in a small pan and cook over a gentle heat, without stirring, until the butter begins to foam. Continue to cook the butter without browning until the foaming stops.
2 Remove the pan from the heat and let it stand until the milky deposits have sunk to the bottom, leaving a clear yellow liquid.
3 Pour this liquid carefully through a double layer of muslin wrung out in warm water into a bowl.
Clarified butter can be stored in a refrigerator for up to 6 weeks and can be used in liquid or solid form.

Leaf Pastry with Drambuie Cream and Strawberries

	METRIC/IMPERIAL	AMERICAN
	150 g/5 oz Puff pastry (opposite)	5 oz Puff pastry (opposite)
	1 egg, size 4, beaten	1 small egg, beaten
Drambuie cream	300 ml/½ pint double cream	1½ cups heavy cream
	1 x 15 ml/1 tablespoon	1 tablespoon superfine
	caster sugar	sugar
	50 ml/2 fl oz Drambuie	4 tablespoons Drambuie
To finish	icing sugar, for dusting	confectioners' (powdered) sugar, for dusting
	200 ml/7 fl oz Raspberry coulis (page 50)	scant cup Raspberry coulis (page 50)
	4-6 large ripe strawberries, thinly sliced	4-6 large strawberries, thinly sliced

Serves 4

Preparation time:
40 minutes,
including
chilling time

Cooking time:
20 minutes

Oven:230°C, 450°F,
Gas Mark 8

1 Roll out the puff pastry to a thickness of 5 mm/¼ inch. Cut out 4 leaf shapes, each about 10 cm/4 inches x 6 cm/2½ inches.
2 Brush the leaves with beaten egg and chill in the refrigerator for 20 minutes.
3 On a non-stick baking sheet, bake the leaves in a preheated oven for about 18-20 minutes. Cool on a rack.
4 To make the Drambuie cream, whip the cream with sugar to taste (remember the Drambuie is sweet), until it stands in soft peaks. Stir in the Drambuie and whisk again to a piping consistency. Fill into a piping (pastry) bag.
5 Carefully slice 5 mm/¼ inch off the top of each pastry leaf, taking care not to damage it. (This slice will be the lid.) Pipe the Drambuie cream into each pastry case. Lay the strawberry slices over the cream. Sift the icing (confectioners') sugar over the lids and set on top of the cream.
6 Pour a little raspberry coulis on to a plate and place a pastry leaf on top.

Leaf Pastry with Drambuie Cream and Strawberries

Puff Pastry

METRIC/IMPERIAL	AMERICAN
225 g/8 oz plain flour	*½ lb (1½ cups) all-purpose flour*
salt	*salt*
225 g/8 oz margarine or butter, very cold	*½ lb margarine or butter, very cold*
150 ml/¼ pint ice-cold water	*generous ½ cup (5 fl oz) ice-cold water*
few drops of lemon juice	*few drops of lemon juice*

Note: care must be taken when rolling out the paste to keep the ends and sides square. The lightness of the paste is caused by the air which is trapped when folding the pastry during preparation.

49

Makes 500 g/
1¼ lb

Preparation time:
20 minutes

Resting time:
1 hour 50 minutes

1 Sift the flour and salt into a bowl. Rub or cut in with a pastry blender, 50 g/2 oz/ 4 tablespoons of the fat.

2 Make a well in the centre and add the water and lemon juice. Knead well into a smooth dough to form a ball. Leave the dough to rest in a cool place for 30 minutes.

3 Cut a cross half way through the dough and pull out the corners to form a star shape. Roll out the points of the star square, leaving the centre thick.

4 Knead the remaining fat to the same texture as the dough. (This is most important: if the fat is too soft it will melt and ooze out, if too hard it will break through the paste when being rolled.)

5 Place the fat on the thick centre of the star shape and fold over the flaps. Roll out to approximately 30 x 15 cm/12 x 6 inches, cover with a cloth and leave to rest in a cool place for 20 minutes.

6 Roll out to approximately 60 x 20 cm/24 x 8 inches, fold both ends into the centre and fold in half again to form a square – this is one double turn. Leave to rest in a cool place for 20 minutes.

7 Half turn the paste to the right or left and roll out again. Give one more double turn (Step 6), roll out and leave to rest for 20 minutes. Give the pastry 2 more double turns, rolling out and resting between each turn. Leave to rest for another 20 minutes before using.

Raspberry Coulis

METRIC/IMPERIAL	AMERICAN
50 ml/ 2 fl oz water	*¼ cup water*
450 g/1 lb fresh or frozen raspberries	*1 lb fresh or frozen raspberries*
75 g/3 oz caster sugar	*6 tablespoons (⅜ cup) superfine or granulated sugar*

1 Bring the water to the boil in a heavy-based pan, add the raspberries and sugar and simmer until very soft.

2 Press the mixture through a conical strainer, transfer to a jam (jelly) bag and leave suspended over a basin until all the juice has drained through. The bag must be supported so that the bottom of it does not dip into the juice in the basin.

3 Pour the clear juice into a small bowl, cover and refrigerate until ready to serve.

Chilled Fennel and Cucumber Soup with Grated Carrot

Chicken, Melon and Pineapple Salad with Raspberry Vinaigrette

Meringue Baskets with Fresh Fruits and Cream

Chilled Fennel and Cucumber Soup with Grated Carrot

METRIC/IMPERIAL	AMERICAN
25 g/1 oz butter	*2 tablespoons butter*
50 g/2 oz onion, peeled and sliced	*1 small onion, peeled and sliced*
50 g/2 oz leek, white part only	*1 leek, white part only*
1.2 litres/2 pints Chicken stock (below)	*2½ pints Chicken stock (below)*
2 small heads fennel, chopped	*2 small heads fennel, chopped*
1 medium cucumber, chopped	*1 medium cucumber, chopped*
salt and pepper	*salt and pepper*
150 ml/¼ pint double cream, chilled	*generous ½ cup heavy cream, chilled*

To garnish

1 large carrot, peeled and grated	*1 large carrot, peeled and grated*
chopped chives	*chopped chives*

Serves 4

Preparation time: 15 minutes

Cooking time: 40 minutes

Chilling time: overnight

1 Melt the butter in a heavy-based pan. Add the onion and leek, cover the pan and sauté for a few minutes, without colouring.

2 Add the stock, fennel and cucumber, bring to the boil and simmer for about 30 minutes until the vegetables are tender.

3 Pass the soup through a sieve, then liquidize the soup.

4 Pour the soup into a clean pan, bring to the boil and adjust the seasoning. Cool, then chill in the refrigerator overnight.

5 To serve, stir in the chilled cream. Pour into individual bowls and garnish with grated carrot and chopped chives.

Chicken Stock

METRIC/IMPERIAL	AMERICAN
1 kg/2 lb raw chicken bones	*2 lb raw chicken bones*
225 g/8 oz vegetables	*½ lb vegetables*
(carrots, onions, celery, leeks)	*(carrots, onions, celery, leeks)*
bouquet garni (thyme, bay leaf, parsley stalks)	*bouquet garni (thyme, bay leaf, parsley stalks)*
6 black peppercorns	*6 black peppercorns*
2 level dessertspoons salt	*4 teaspoons salt*

Makes 1.75 litres/ 3 pints/ 4 pints (US)

Cooking time: 2-3 hours

Oven: 220°C, 425° F, Gas Mark 7

1 Chop the bones and brown well on all sides by one of 2 methods: a) place in a roasting tin in a preheated oven for 45 minutes, or b) brown carefully for 10 minutes in a little fat in a frying pan.

2 Drain off any fat and put the bones in a stock pot. Set the roasting tin or frying pan over high heat, and brown the remaining sediment, scraping it from the bottom of the pan with a wooden spoon. Pour in 300 ml/½ pint/1/¼ cups of water and simmer for a few minutes, then add to the bones. Do not discard the water. Add 2.25 litres/4 pints/5 pints (US) water. Bring to the boil and skim well.

3 Wash, peel and roughly chop the vegetables and gently fry in a little hot oil or fat until brown. Strain off the fat and add the vegetables to the stock pot. Add the bouquet garni, peppercorns and salt and simmer for 6-8 hours (2 hours for chicken stock). Skim off any froth that rises to the top from time to time. At the end of the cooking time, skim again thoroughly, strain and cool. This stock will keep 3-4 days in a refrigerator, or 2 months if frozen.

Chicken, Melon and Pineapple Salad with Raspberry Vinaigrette

	METRIC/IMPERIAL	AMERICAN
	1 galia melon, peeled and quartered	1 galia or honeydew melon, peeled and quartered
	4 small cooked chicken breasts	4 small cooked chicken breasts
	8 small chicory spears	4 small endive
	½ small pineapple, peeled	½ small pineapple, peeled
Vinaigrette	50 ml/2 fl oz olive oil	¼ cup olive oil
	3 dessertspoons raspberry vinegar	4 teaspoons raspberry vinegar
	1 shallot, finely chopped	1 shallot, finely chopped
	salt and pepper	salt and pepper
To garnish	4 cherry tomatoes	4 cherry tomatoes
	4 small bunches of cress	bunch of watercress, well washed

Serves 4

Preparation time: 20 minutes

1 For each serving, cut one quarter of melon into thin slices, and form into a fan on one side of a dinner plate.

2 Cut one chicken breast into 6 even-sized pieces and place on the other side of the plate.

3 Place 2 spears of chicory (endive) at the top of the plate behind the chicken.

4 Carefully cut out all pineapple 'eyes' and cut into quarters.

5 Lay each pineapple quarter horizontally on a plate and cut it into thin slices, about 3mm/⅛ inch thick, holding the knife at a 45 degree angle. Place 6 thin slices of pineapple on each plate between the melon and the chicken.

6 To make the vinaigrette, mix together the olive oil, raspberry vinegar, shallot and salt and pepper. Serve separately in a small dish or jug (pitcher).

7 Cut each cherry tomato in slices from base to top, almost but not all the way through, so that it can be fanned out.

8 Place a little cress (watercress) and a fanned-out tomato on each plate.

Meringue Baskets with Fresh Fruits and Cream

	METRIC/IMPERIAL	AMERICAN
Meringue	2 egg whites, size 1	2 jumbo egg whites
	100 g/4 oz caster sugar	generous ½ cup superfine sugar
Filling	250 ml/8 fl oz double cream	1 cup heavy cream
	15 g/½ oz caster sugar	1 level tablespoon superfine or granulated sugar
	1 star fruit, cut into 8 slices*	1 star fruit, cut into 8 slices*
	1 kiwi fruit, cut into 8 slices	1 kiwi fruit, cut into 8 slices
	4 black grapes, halved and seeded	4 black grapes, halved and seeded
	4 green grapes, halved and seeded	4 green grapes, halved and seeded
	4 large strawberries	4 large strawberries
Sauce	½ recipe Raspberry coulis (page 54)	½ recipe Raspberry coulis (page 54)

*If star fruit is not available, use any tropical soft fruit (pomegranates, grenadillas, etc).

Chilled Fennel and Cucumber Soup with Grated Carrot
Chicken, Melon and Pineapple Salad with Raspberry Vinaigrette

Serves 4

Preparation time:
about 20 minutes

Cooking time:
4 hours

Oven: 110°C, 225°F,
Gas Mark ¼

1 To make the meringue, place the egg whites and sugar in a glass bowl and set over a pan of hot water. Stir until the sugar has dissolved.

2 Whisk vigorously until the mixture forms stiff, glossy peaks.

3 Place the meringue mixture in a piping (pastry) bag fitted with a plain 1 cm/ ½ inch nozzle.

4 On a piece of greaseproof (waxed) paper, draw 4 circles approximately 10 cm/ 4 inches in diameter. Pipe a border of meringue around the outside edge of each circle, and continue to pipe in ever-decreasing circles until a complete base is formed. The meringue should be about 1 cm/½ inch thick.

5 Place the meringues on a baking (cookie) sheet in a preheated oven and bake for 4 hours or until dry. Remove from the oven and peel off the paper. Set the meringues carefully on a rack and leave to cool completely.

6 To prepare the filling, mix together the double (heavy) cream and sugar and whisk until thick. Spoon or pipe the cream on to the meringue bases, making a slight hollow in the centre.

7 Decorate each meringue basket with 2 slices of star fruit (or other tropical soft fruit), 2 slices of kiwi fruit, 2 halves of black and green grapes and 1 strawberry.

8 Divide the sauce between 4 dessert plates. Place a meringue basket in the centre, on top of the sauce.

Raspberry Coulis

METRIC/IMPERIAL	AMERICAN
50 ml/ 2 fl oz water	*¼ cup water*
450 g/1 lb fresh or frozen raspberries	*1 lb fresh or frozen raspberries*
75 g/3 oz caster sugar	*6 tablespoons (⅜ cup) superfine or granulated sugar*

Makes 300 ml/
½ pint/1¼ cups

Preparation time:
30 minutes

1 Bring the water to the boil in a heavy-based pan, add the raspberries and sugar and simmer until very soft.

2 Press the mixture through a conical strainer, transfer to a jam (jelly) bag and leave suspended over a basin until all the juice has drained through. The bag must be supported so that the bottom of it does not dip into the juice in the basin.

3 Pour the clear juice into a small bowl, cover and refrigerate until ready to serve.

Sweet Peppers filled with Fine Vegetable Mousse and Fresh Tomato Sauce

*Asparagus and Artichoke Quiches with Spinach
   and Courgette (Zucchini) Sauce*

*Sliced Banana and Strawberries with Honey Ice Cream
   and Chocolate Sauce*

Sweet Peppers Filled with Fine Vegetable Mousse and Fresh Tomato Sauce

METRIC/IMPERIAL	AMERICAN
250 ml/8 fl oz double cream	*1 cup heavy cream*
7.5 ml/1½ teaspoons liquid honey	*1½ teaspoons liquid honey*
75 g/3 oz cooked carrot purée	*½ cup cooked carrot purée*
75 g/3 oz cooked broccoli purée	*½ cup cooked broccoli purée*
10 g/2 level teaspoons powdered gelatine	*2 level teaspoons powdered gelatin*
1 medium green pepper	*1 medium green pepper*
1 medium red pepper	*1 medium red pepper*
salt and pepper	*salt and pepper*

To serve

250 ml/8 fl oz Tomato coulis (below)	*1 cup Tomato coulis (below)*
1 large carrot, peeled and cut into thin strips	*1 large carrot, peeled and cut into thin strips*
chervil sprigs	*chervil sprigs*

Serves 4

Preparation time: 15 minutes

Chilling time: overnight

1 Divide the cream between 2 saucepans and bring to the boil. Stir the honey into the carrot purée and add to one pan. Stir the broccoli purée into the other pan. Remove from the heat and pour into separate bowls. Dissolve the gelatine in 2 tablespoons of hot water. Stir until completely clear. Stir half into the carrot purée and the other half into the broccoli mixture.

2 Carefully cut the tops from the peppers and scrape out the seeds with the back of a spoon, without breaking the shells. Rinse and dry. Stand the pepper shells pointed-end down in an egg tray or deep muffin tins.

3 When the vegetable mixtures are cooled but not set, fill the red pepper with the broccoli cream and the green pepper with the carrot cream. Stand each pepper upright in a coffee mug and leave to set in the refrigerator overnight.

4 Lay the peppers on their sides on a plate and cut into 4 slices approximately 5 mm/¼ inch thick.

5 To serve, pour a little tomato coulis on each of 4 plates. Lay a slice of green and a slice of red pepper on top of the sauce, garnish with a few carrot strips and a sprig of chervil on each plate.

Tomato Coulis

METRIC/IMPERIAL	AMERICAN
25 g/1 oz butter	*2 tablespoons butter*
¼ medium onion, chopped	*1 small onion, chopped*
3 basil leaves, chopped	*3 basil leaves, chopped*
10 tomatoes, roughly chopped	*10 tomatoes, roughly chopped*
few drops of Tabasco	*few drops of Tabasco*
1 x 2.5 ml spoon/½ teaspoon Worcestershire sauce	*½ teaspoon Worcestershire sauce*
salt and pepper	*salt and pepper*

Makes 600 ml/ 1 pint/1¼ pints (US)

1 Melt the butter in a pan, add the onion and chopped basil and cook gently for a few minutes.

2 Add the tomatoes, cover the pan and cook for about 15 minutes until very soft.

3 Pour the mixture into a liquidizer, add the sauces and blend well. Season.

4 Strain the sauce through a fine sieve to remove all skin and seeds. Leave to cool.

Sweet Peppers filled with Fine Vegetable Mousse and Fresh Tomato Sauce
Asparagus and Artichoke Quiche with Courgette (Zucchini) Sauce

Asparagus and Artichoke Quiches with Spinach and Courgette (Zucchini) Sauce

	METRIC/IMPERIAL	AMERICAN
Shortcrust pastry	175 g/6 oz plain flour	1¼ cups all-purpose flour
	pinch of salt	pinch of salt
	75 g/3 oz margarine,	6 tablespoons margarine,
	very cold	very cold
	water, for mixing	water, for mixing
Filling	4 canned artichoke bottoms,	4 canned artichoke bottoms,
	thinly sliced	thinly sliced
	8 asparagus tips, cut into	8 asparagus tips, cut into
	2.5-4 cm/1-1½ inch lengths	1-1½ inch lengths
	salt and pepper	salt and pepper
	4 eggs, size 1, beaten	4 jumbo eggs, beaten
	175 ml/6 fl oz milk	¾ cup milk
	120 ml/4 fl oz double cream	½ cup heavy cream

	METRIC/IMPERIAL	AMERICAN
Sauce	15 g/½ oz butter	*1 tablespoon butter*
	1 small onion (about 100 g/	*1 small onion, roughly*
	4 oz), roughly chopped	*chopped*
	1 small courgette, roughly chopped	*1 small zucchini, roughly chopped*
	4 fresh spinach leaves, washed	*4 fresh spinach leaves, washed*
	175 ml/6 fl oz double cream	*¾ cup heavy cream*
	50 ml/2 fl oz vegetable stock	*¼ cup vegetable stock*
	(may be made from a cube)	*(may be made from a stock cube)*
	pinch of nutmeg	*pinch of nutmeg*
	salt and pepper	*salt and pepper*

Serves 4

Preparation time:
20 minutes

Cooking time:
35 minutes

Oven: 200°C, 400°F,
Gas Mark 6

1 To make the pastry, sift the flour and salt into a bowl and rub or cut in the fat, until the mixture resembles breadcrumbs. Add enough cold water to form a dough.
2 Grease four 10 cm/4 inch diameter individual flan cases and line with the pastry. Divide the artichoke and asparagus pieces evenly between the cases and season.
3 Mix the milk and cream with the beaten eggs and strain into a bowl. Pour into the flan cases and bake in a preheated oven for about 15-20 minutes.
4 While the quiches are cooking, make the sauce. Melt the butter in a heavy-based pan and gently cook the onion, spinach and courgettes (zucchini) for 2-3 minutes. Stir in the cream, vegetable stock and nutmeg, then bring to the boil and simmer until the vegetables are tender – about 5 minutes. Liquidize, adjust the seasoning to taste and strain.
5 Pour a little of the sauce on to each plate and place a quiche in the centre.

Sliced Banana and Strawberries with Honey Ice Cream and Chocolate Sauce

	METRIC/IMPERIAL	AMERICAN
	2 bananas	*2 bananas*
	25 g/1 oz desiccated coconut	*½ cup (level) unsweetened coconut*
	16 strawberries	*16 strawberries*
	4 sprigs of mint	*4 sprigs of mint*
Chocolate sauce	100 g/4 oz grated milk dessert chocolate	*4 oz semi-sweet chocolate*
	85 ml/3 fl oz warm milk	*scant ½ cup (3 fl oz) warm milk*
Honey ice cream	100 g/4 oz caster sugar	*8 tablespoons superfine or granulated sugar*
	4 egg yolks, size 1	*4 jumbo egg yolks*
	few drops of vanilla essence	*few drops of vanilla extract*
	450 ml/¾ pint milk	*scant pint (15 fl oz) milk*
	150 ml/¼ pint double cream	*generous ½ cup heavy cream*
	50 g/2 oz runny honey	*3 tablespoons liquid honey*

Serves 4

Preparation time:
20 minutes

Cooking time:
about 15 minutes

Freezing time:
4 hours

1 To make the ice cream, whisk the sugar, egg yolks and vanilla essence together in a bowl until light and fluffy.
2 Boil the milk and whisk it into the mixture. Add the honey and mix well.
3 Pour the mixture into a heavy-based pan and stir over a low heat until the mixture coats the back of a spoon. Strain and leave to cool completely.
4 When cool, stir in the double (heavy) cream and freeze in an ice cream machine, following the manufacturers' instructions, until fairly firm. Remove from the machine and store in a covered container in a deep freeze or freezing compartment of a refrigerator.
5 To make the chocolate sauce, melt the chocolate in a bowl over hot water. Add the warmed milk, stirring constantly, until thoroughly mixed. Keep warm over a bowl of hot water.
6 Slice the bananas and roll them in the coconut. Divide between 4 glass coupe-shaped dishes.
7 Place a ball of honey ice cream on the bananas; top with 3 sliced strawberries.
8 Pour some warm chocolate sauce over the top and decorate each dish with one whole strawberry and a sprig of mint. Serve immediately, before the ice cream starts to melt.

Mediterranean Prawns (Shrimp) with Sweet Chilli Sauce

Apple Mint Sorbet

Vegetables Wrapped in Filo Pastry with a Cream Broccoli Sauce

Lemon Meringue Pie

Mediterranean Prawns (Shrimp) with Sweet Chilli Sauce

	METRIC/IMPERIAL	AMERICAN
Sweet chilli sauce	150 ml/¼ pint Tomato coulis (page 55)	*generous ½ cup (about 5 fl oz) Tomato coulis (page 55)*
	1 dessertspoon creamed horseradish sauce	*1 tablespoon sour cream and about 1 teaspoon bottled horseradish, drained**
	1 x 5 ml spoon/1 heaped teaspoon chopped chives	*1 heaped teaspoon chopped chives*
	1 Kenyan chilli pepper, seeded and finely chopped	*1 jalapeno pepper or serrano pepper (very hot), seeded and finely chopped*
	25 ml/1 fl oz liquid honey	*1½ tablespoons honey*
	20 Mediterranean prawns, cooked	*20 large shrimp, cooked*
	4-6 sprigs of dill	*4-6 sprigs of dill*

*Bottled horseradish varies greatly in strength, so it should be added to the sour cream by teaspoons, to the desired flavour.

Serves 4

Preparation time: 10 minutes

Chilling time: overnight

1 Mix the tomato coulis, horseradish sauce (sour cream mixed with bottled horse-radish sauce), chives, chillies and honey in a glass or stainless steel bowl. Cover and refrigerate overnight to allow the flavours to blend.

2 Peel off the prawn (shrimp) tails, leaving the heads intact. Arrange 5 prawns on each plate, tails toward the middle and heads fanned out around the perimeter.

3 Spoon 2 tablespoons of sweet chilli sauce over the tails, allowing some of the sauce to flow on to the plate. Garnish each portion with a sprig of dill.

Apple Mint Sorbet

	METRIC/IMPERIAL	AMERICAN
	1 large sprig fresh apple mint	*1 large sprig fresh apple mint*
	100 ml/3½ fl oz boiling water	*7 tablespoons boiling water*
	250 ml/8 fl oz Stock syrup (page 28)	*1 cup Stock syrup (page 28)*
	1 egg white, size 4, lightly beaten	*1 small egg white, lightly beaten*

Serves 4

Preparation time: about 8 minutes

Freezing time: about 30-35 minutes

1 Strip the apple mint leaves from their stem and infuse them in the boiling water for 5 minutes. Leave to cool.

2 Mix the liquid with the stock syrup and pour into a sorbet machine or ice-cream maker and freeze, following the manufacturers' instructions, for 15 – 20 minutes until it is slushy.

3 Add the egg white, mix thoroughly and continue to freeze until a sorbet consistency is reached.

4 Place the sorbet in a piping (pastry) bag fitted with a star nozzle and pipe into individual ramekin dishes.

Vegetables Wrapped in Filo Pastry with a Cream Broccoli Sauce

METRIC/IMPERIAL	AMERICAN
40 g/1½ oz butter	*3 tablespoons butter*
1 medium onion, peeled and roughly chopped	*1 medium onion, peeled and roughly chopped*
1 carrot, half-boiled and roughly chopped	*1 carrot, half-boiled and roughly chopped*
½ small cauliflower, divided into florets	*½ small cauliflower, divided into florets*
½ green pepper, cored, seeded and roughly chopped	*½ green pepper, cored, seeded and roughly chopped*
½ red pepper, cored, seeded and roughly chopped	*½ red pepper, cored, seeded and roughly chopped*
1 medium courgette, roughly chopped	*1 medium zucchini, roughly chopped*
5 ears baby corn	*5 ears baby corn*
2 large, ripe tomatoes, peeled, seeded and chopped	*2 large, ripe tomatoes, peeled, seeded and chopped*
1 garlic clove, crushed	*1 garlic clove, crushed*
50 ml/2 fl oz carrot juice	*4 tablespoons carrot juice*
few drops of Worcestershire sauce	*few drops of Worcestershire sauce*
few drops of Tabasco sauce	*few drops of Tabasco or any hot pepper sauce*
salt and pepper	*salt and pepper*
chopped parsley	*chopped parsley*

Sauce

METRIC/IMPERIAL	AMERICAN
135 ml/4½ fl oz vegetable stock	*generous ½ cup vegetable stock*
200-225 g fresh broccoli, head only	*½ lb fresh broccoli, head only*
200 ml/⅓ pint double cream	*⅞ cup heavy cream*
pinch of nutmeg	*pinch of nutmeg*

Pastry

METRIC/IMPERIAL	AMERICAN
8 sheets filo pastry	*8 sheets filo or strudel pastry*
40 g/1½ oz sesame seeds	*1 rounded tablespoon sesame seeds*

Serves 4

Preparation time: 30 minutes

Cooking time: 40 minutes

Oven: 230°C, 450° F, Gas Mark 8

1 Melt the butter in a heavy-based pan, add the onion, carrots and cauliflower florets and cook, without colouring, for 3-4 minutes.

2 Add the peppers, courgettes (zucchini), baby corn and garlic and continue cooking, stirring frequently, for another 5 minutes. Add the carrot juice, sauces and salt and pepper.

3 Cover the pan and simmer over a low heat for about 5 minutes or until the ingredients are cooked 'al dente' (i.e. still have a bite to them). Stir in the tomatoes, remove from the heat, pour into a bowl and leave to cool. Adjust the seasoning, stir in the parsley, mixing well.

4 To make the sauce, bring the vegetable stock to the boil, add the broccoli and cook for 6-8 minutes until tender. Add the cream and nutmeg and continue cooking for a further 15 minutes. Liquidize the mixture, then strain into a clean pan, and re-heat for a further 10 minutes while you prepare the pastry.

5 Lay out 2 sheets of pastry, one on top of the other. Keep the remaining sheets covered with a well wrung-out damp cloth until used, as they begin to dry out and crack almost immediately. Spoon about 45 ml/3 tablespoons of the vegetable mixture into the centre and fold in the sides then fold over the ends, to overlap and form a secure parcel about 10 cm/4 inches square. Repeat for all 8 parcels.

6 Turn the parcels over, brush with a little water and sprinkle with sesame seeds. Bake in a preheated oven for approximately 12-15 minutes.

7 Pour a little sauce on to each plate and place a vegetable parcel in the centre.

Lemon Meringue Pie

METRIC/IMPERIAL

AMERICAN

	METRIC/IMPERIAL	AMERICAN
Pastry	1 egg, size 4, beaten	*1 small egg, beaten*
	50 g/2 oz butter	*4 tablespoons butter*
	20 g/¾ oz caster sugar	*1½ tablespoons superfine sugar*
	75 g/3 oz plain flour, sieved	*½ cup (3 oz) flour, sieved*
	1 x 5 ml spoon/1 teaspoon cold water, if necessary	*1 teaspoon cold water, if necessary*
Filling	1 x 15 ml spoon/1 tablespoon water	*1 tablespoon water*
	40 g/1½ oz caster sugar	*3 tablespoons superfine sugar*
	1 x 5 ml spoon/1 teaspoon cornflour	*1 teaspoon cornstarch*
	15 g/½ oz butter	*1 tablespoon butter*
	juice and zest of ½ small lemon	*juice and zest of ½ small lemon*
	2 egg yolks, size 3, beaten	*2 small egg yolks, beaten*
Meringue	2 egg whites, size 4, beaten	*2 small egg whites, beaten*
	75 g/3 oz caster sugar	*6 tablespoons superfine sugar*

Serves 4

Preparation time: 40 minutes

Cooking time: 15 minutes

Setting time: 2 hours

Oven: 120°C, 250° F, Gas Mark ½ then: 240°C, 475° F, Gas Mark 9

1 To make the pastry, cream the egg, butter and sugar in a bowl, add the flour and mix to a smooth paste. Add a little water if the mixture is too dry. Roll out.

2 Grease a 23 cm/9 inch flan tin, 2.5 cm/1 inch deep, and line with the pastry. Place in a preheated oven and bake for 12 minutes or until golden brown. Leave to cool.

3 To make the filling, boil the water and sugar to a syrup in a heavy-based pan. Place the cornflour (cornstarch) in a small bowl and stir in a little of the syrup to make a smooth paste. Gradually stir this back into the syrup and blend until smooth.

4 Remove from the heat and stir in the butter, lemon juice and zest until complelely mixed. Pour a little of the hot mixture into the bowl of beaten egg yolks and mix well, then whisk back into the remaining lemon mixture. Pour the filling into the flan case and leave to set, about 2 hours.

5 To make the meringue, place the beaten egg whites and sugar in a glass bowl. Set it over a pan of hot water, and stir constantly until the sugar has dissolved.

6 Whisk until the meringue forms stiff peaks. Place the mixture in a piping (pastry) bag fitted with a 1 cm/½ inch star nozzle. Pipe the meringue in a decorative pattern on top of the pie.

7 Increase the oven temperature and bake the pie for 2 minutes until the meringue is golden brown. Allow to cool before serving.

Outside The Dormy House overlooking the King's Golf Course: Lemon Meringue Pie

Fanned Melon with Fresh Berries and Apple Mint Yogurt

METRIC/IMPERIAL	AMERICAN
2 small galia melons	*2 small galia or honeydew melons*
250 ml/8 fl oz natural yogurt	*1 cup plain, unflavored yogurt*
100 ml/3½ fl oz apple mint liqueur	*scant ½ cup apple mint liqueur*
12 large strawberries,	*12 large strawberries, cut*
cut in half	*in half*
4 sprigs of mint	*4 sprigs of mint*

Serves 4

**Preparation time:
15 minutes**

1 Peel the melons and cut in half vertically. Scoop out the seeds.

2 Cut each half into quarters, so that you have 8 pieces. Lay a quarter on its side with the top away from you and the base toward you. Holding a sharp knife horizontally, make an incision 5 mm/¼ inch deep right through the melon, but only two-thirds along the length. Repeat the process at 5 mm/¼ inch intervals. Press down lightly on the top of the melon to make it fan out. Repeat with the remaining pieces.

3 Blend the yogurt with the liqueur.

4 Place two fanned-out quarters of melon on a plate, one to the left and one to the right. Pour a little yogurt sauce into the gap at the front. On the other side of the plate, place 6 of the halved strawberries. Decorate with a sprig of mint.

Broiled Salmon Steak with Pike Mousse and Chives

	METRIC/IMPERIAL	AMERICAN
Pike mousse	225 g/8 oz pike meat	*½ lb pike meat, fresh or frozen*
	300 ml/½ pint double cream	*1¼ cups heavy cream*
	salt and pepper	*salt and pepper*
	1 x 15 ml spoon/1 tablespoon	*1 tablespoon chopped*
	chopped chives	*chives*
	4 x 225 g/8 oz salmon steaks	*4 x ½ lb salmon steaks*
	1 large carrot, peeled and	*1 large carrot, peeled and*
	finely shredded	*finely shredded*
	1 small leek, well washed	*1 small leek, well washed*
	(white part only), finely	*(white part only), finely*
	shredded	*shredded*
	1 large stick celery,	*1 large stick celery,*
	trimmed and finely shredded	*trimmed and finely shredded*
	175 ml/6 fl oz cold Fish stock	*¾ cup cold Fish stock*
	(opposite)	*(opposite)*

Serves 4

**Preparation time:
30 minutes**

**Cooking time:
20 minutes**

**Oven: 230°C, 450°F,
Gas Mark 8**

1 To make the pike mousse, pick out and discard any bones and skin from the pike meat. Mince (grind) it finely and put in a bowl set in a larger bowl of crushed ice. Chill thoroughly.

2 Beat the cream into the minced (ground) pike in even stages until completely incorporated. Adjust the seasoning to taste and mix in the chopped chives.

3 Remove the centre bones from the salmon steaks and fill the cavities with pike mousse. Place the steaks in a lightly buttered ovenproof dish, into which they will fit snugly. Sprinkle with the shredded vegetables and season. Pour the cold fish stock over. Cover the dish and bake in a preheated oven for 15-20 minutes.

4 Serve the steaks with or without the skin as you like. Béarnaise sauce (page 64) makes an ideal accompaniment.

Fanned Melon with Fresh Berries and Apple Mint Yogurt

Broiled Salmon Steak with Pike Mousse and Chives

Fish Stock

METRIC/IMPERIAL

25 g/1 oz butter or margarine
100 g/4 oz onions, peeled and sliced
1 kg/2 lb white fish bones (preferably
sole, whiting, turbot, etc), viscera
and gills removed
1 bay leaf
juice of ½ small lemon
parsley stalks
3 peppercorns
2.25 litres/4 pints water

AMERICAN

2 tablespoons butter or margarine
1 medium onion, peeled and sliced
2 lb white fish bones from any non-
oily fish (flounder, sole, whiting,
weakfish), viscera and gills removed
1 bay leaf
juice of ½ a small lemon
parsley stalks
3 peppercorns
5 pints water

Makes 1.75 litres/
3 pints/3¾ pints (US)

Preparation time:
10 minutes

Cooking time:
30 minutes

1 Melt the butter or margarine in a very large heavy-based pan. Add the onions,
fish bones and all the other ingredients except the water. Cover the pan with
greaseproof (waxed) paper and a lid and cook gently for 5 minutes.
2 Remove the paper and add the water. Bring to the boil, skim and simmer for 20
minutes only. Strain and cool.
3 Chill in the refrigerator, where it will keep for 2-3 days. Fish stock can be frozen
for up to 1 month.

Béarnaise Sauce

METRIC/IMPERIAL

AMERICAN

2 shallots, chopped
2 x 15 ml spoons/2 tablespoons
tarragon vinegar
15 g/½ oz chopped
tarragon leaves
10 peppercorns, crushed
4 egg yolks, size 1, beaten
350 g/12 oz Clarified butter,
melted and cooled to tepid (page 48)
1 dessertspoon chopped
parsley

2 shallots, chopped
2 tablespoons tarragon
vinegar
1½ teaspoons chopped
tarragon leaves
10 peppercorns, crushed
4 jumbo egg yolks, beaten
1½ cups Clarified butter,
melted and cooled to tepid (page 48)
1 rounded teaspoon chopped
parsley

Makes generous
450 ml/15 fl oz/
scant pint (US)

Preparation time:
5 minutes

1 Place the shallots, vinegar, tarragon, and peppercorns in a heavy-based pan. Bring to the boil and reduce by half. Leave to cool.
2 Add the egg yolks and whisk over a bowl of hot water until light and fluffy. Remove from the heat and gradually add the melted butter, whisking all the time. If the sauce becomes too thick, add a little hot water.
3 Strain into a clean bowl and add the parsley. Serve the sauce warm.

Cooking time: approximately 8-10 minutes

Chilled Grand Marnier Soufflé

METRIC/IMPERIAL

AMERICAN

2 egg yolks, size 1
40 g/1½ oz caster sugar
zest of 2 oranges
300 ml/½ pint double cream, softly
whipped
2 measures (50 ml/2 fl oz)
Grand Marnier

2 jumbo egg yolks
3 tablespoons superfine sugar
zest of 2 oranges
1¼ cups heavy cream, softly
whipped
4 tablespoons Grand Marnier

Crystallized
(candied)
lime shreds

2 limes
75 g/3 oz caster sugar
150 ml/¼ pint water

2 limes
6 tablespoons superfine sugar
½ cup (5 fl oz) water

Serves 4

Preparation time:
15 minutes

Freezing time:
overnight

1 Place the egg yolks, sugar and orange zest in a glass bowl. Stand it in a deeper bowl of hot water, or over the base of a double boiler half-filled with simmering water, and whisk until the mixture is light and fluffy.
2 In a separate bowl half-whip the double (heavy) cream until it forms soft, not stiff, peaks.
3 Remove the egg and sugar mixture from the hot water and fold in the softly whipped cream. Add half the Grand Marnier and mix lightly but thoroughly.
4 Divide the mixture evenly between 4 individual 7.5 cm/3 inch soufflé dishes, cover with freezer film and place in the freezer overnight.
5 To prepare the crystallized (candied) lime shreds, peel the limes with a vegetable peeler or stripper, making sure that none of the white pith clings to the peel. Cut the skin into hair-thin strips of even size.
6 Mix the water and 50 g/2 oz/4 tablespoons sugar in a heavy-based pan and bring to the boil. Add the strips of lime peel and boil for a further 5 minutes.
7 Remove the lime peel from the syrup and drain well in a fine sieve. Place the remaining sugar in a jar with a tight lid, add the lime peel, cover and shake vigorously, until all the lime strips are coated with the sugar. Drop the lime shreds into a clean, dry sieve, shake to remove any excess sugar and spread on a plate to dry thoroughly.
8 When the Grand Marnier soufflés are frozen, scoop out a small teaspoonful of the mixture from one side of each and set it on top of the soufflé. Just before serving, trickle the remaining Grand Marnier into the cavities. Sprinkle the top of the soufflés with the crystallized (candied) lime shreds.

Scottish Pancakes

Plain and Cinnamon Scones

Almond Slice

Fresh Fruit Tartlets

Scottish Pancakes

METRIC/IMPERIAL	AMERICAN
1 egg, size 1, beaten	*1 jumbo egg, beaten*
50 g/2 oz caster sugar	*4 tablespoons superfine or granulated sugar*
120 ml/4 fl oz milk	*½ cup milk*
1 x 15 ml spoon/1 tablespoon vegetable oil	*1 tablespoon vegetable oil*
150 g/5 oz plain flour	*1 cup (unsifted) all-purpose flour*
15 g/½ oz (2 level teaspoons) baking powder	*2 level teaspoons baking powder*

Makes 20

Preparation time: 5 minutes

Cooking time: about 10 minutes

1 Beat together the egg and sugar until light and fluffy.

2 Add the milk and oil and beat well.

3 Sift the flour and baking powder together and whisk into the liquid.

4 Heat a griddle until a drop of cold water will dance and bounce on the surface without evaporating. Rub with a lightly oiled cloth. Drop a dessertspoon (heaped teaspoon) of the batter on the griddle. When bubbles appear on the top, turn with a palette knife (spatula) and cook for 1 minute more. (Several pancakes can be cooked on the griddle at one time.)

5 Repeat until all the mixture is used up. Keep the pancakes warm between two tea towels.

Plain and Cinnamon Scones

METRIC/IMPERIAL	AMERICAN
350 g/12 oz plain flour	*2¼ cups all-purpose flour*
20 g/¾ oz baking powder	*1½ teaspoons baking powder*
75 g/3 oz butter	*6 tablespoons butter*
175 ml/6 fl oz milk	*¾ cup milk*
75 g/3 oz caster sugar	*6 tablespoons superfine or granulated sugar*
1 x 5 ml/1 heaped teaspoon ground cinnamon	*1 heaped teaspoon ground cinnamon*
milk, for brushing	*milk, for brushing*

Makes 12

Preparation time: 10 minutes

Baking time: 15-20 minutes

Oven: 150°C, 300°F, Gas Mark 2

1 Sieve (sift) the flour and baking powder into a bowl. Rub or cut in the butter until the mixture resembles breadcrumbs.

2 Stir in the milk and sugar and mix lightly. When all the ingredients are half mixed in, divide the mixture between 2 bowls. Add the cinnamon to one bowl and mix to form a dough. Finish mixing the other half to form the same consistency.

3 On a floured board, roll out or pat the doughs, separately, to a thickness of 1 cm/½ inch. Using a 6 cm/2½ inch pastry cutter, cut out rounds and place on a greased baking (cookie) sheet.

4 Brush the tops with milk and bake in a preheated oven for 15-20 minutes.

Almond Slice

METRIC/IMPERIAL	AMERICAN
225 g/8 oz Sweet pastry (opposite)	½ lb Sweet pastry (opposite)
100 g/4 oz butter	8 tablespoons butter
100 g/4 oz caster sugar	½ cup superfine or granulated sugar
2 eggs, size 1, beaten	2 jumbo eggs, beaten
100 g/4 oz ground almonds	1 cup ground almonds
15 g/½ oz (2 tablespoons) plain flour	2 tablespoons all-purpose flour

Yields 8 portions

Preparation time: 10 minutes

Cooking time: 30-35 minutes

Oven: 180°C, 350°F, Gas Mark 4; then: 150°C, 300°F, Gas Mark 2

1 Lightly grease a 30 x 20 cm/12 x 8 inch baking tin, about 1 cm/½ inch deep.

2 Roll out the pastry to a thickness of 3 mm/1/8 inch and line the baking tin. Prick the pastry with a fork and line with a lightly buttered sheet of foil weighed down with dry beans. Place in a preheated oven and bake blind for 3-4 minutes (prick the pastry base with a fork and line with a lightly buttered sheet of foil weighed down with dry beans). Remove from the oven and allow to cool slightly. Reduce the oven temperature.

3 While the pastry is baking, make the filling: beat the butter and sugar together until light and fluffy. Beat in the eggs, then lightly fold in the almonds and the flour.

4 Fill the pastry case with the almond mixture. Bake at the reduced temperature for 25-30 minutes. Leave to cool before cutting into even-sized oblongs.

Sweet Pastry

METRIC/IMPERIAL	AMERICAN
65 g/2½ oz butter	*2 oz plus 2 tablespoons butter*
25 g/1 oz caster sugar	*2 tablespoons superfine sugar*
½ egg, size 4, beaten	*1 very small egg, beaten*
100 g/4 oz flour	*1 cup all-purpose flour*

Makes 225 g/8 oz

1 Cream together the butter and sugar.
2 Add the egg gradually, then mix in the flour to form a dough.
3 Chill for 30 minutes before rolling out.

Fresh Fruit Tartlets

METRIC/IMPERIAL	AMERICAN
175 g/6 oz Sweet pastry (above)	*1 recipe Sweet pastry (above)*
300 ml/½ pint double cream	*1½ cups heavy cream*
40 g/1½ oz caster sugar	*2½ tablespoons superfine sugar*
3 drops of vanilla essence	*3 drops of vanilla extract*

To decorate

40 raspberries	*40 raspberries*
8 large strawberries, sliced	*8 large strawberries, sliced*
8 blueberries	*8 blueberries*
2 kiwi fruit, peeled and sliced	*2 kiwi fruit, peeled and sliced*
12 orange segments	*12 orange segments*
4 grapes	*4 grapes*
8 mint leaves	*8 mint leaves*

Makes 12

Preparation time: 15 minutes

Cooking time: 6-8 minutes

Oven: 120°C, 250°F, Gas Mark ½

1 Roll out the pastry thinly to a thickness of about 3 mm/⅛ inch. Using a 9 cm/3½ inch diameter cutter, stamp out 12 rounds. Gently ease the pastry rounds into a 12-hole bun tin. Chill the pastry shells (in the bun tin) for 30 minutes.
2 Prick the pastry bases with a fork, place in a preheated oven and bake unfilled for 6-8 minutes. Remove from the oven, allow the pastry to cool in the tins for a few minutes, then carefully remove.
3 Whisk the cream, sugar and vanilla essence (extract) until thick but not stiff. Divide evenly between the tartlet cases.
4 Decorate 4 tartlets with raspberries, 4 with a combination of strawberries and blueberries and the remaining 4 with kiwi fruit, orange segments and grapes. Garnish the raspberry and strawberry tartlets with mint leaves.

Scottish Pancakes
Almond Slice
Plain and Cinnamon Scones
Fresh Fruit Tartlets

AUTUMN

*The season of changing colours and falling
leaves is nowhere more beautiful than in Scotland,
with its purple heather and rolling mists.*

*In Autumn Gleneagles comes into its own: conditions
are ideal for horseriding, clay target shooting,
playing golf, or rambling through the countryside.*

*The Autumn recipes, devised to satisfy hearty outdoor
appetites, feature wholesome, filling food.
Here you will find warming soups and broths, savoury
breads and chunky pâtés. Oysters and mussels
are a special Autumn treat, as are harvest fruits,
such as crunchy apples and sweet dessert pears.
Duck, pigeon and venison make a welcome
appearance in the menus.*

*The Autumn menu selection ensures that the bountiful
fruits of this mellow season can be enjoyed to the full.*

Oysters, Mediterranean Prawns (Shrimp) and Marinated Mussels with a Spiced Cocktail Sauce

METRIC/IMPERIAL	AMERICAN
75 g/3 oz Atlantic seaweed, if available	*small handful of fresh seaweed, if available*
750 ml/1¼ pints water	*1½ pints water*
16 medium-sized mussels	*16 medium mussels*

Marinade

85 ml/3 fl oz Fish stock (opposite)	*6 tablespoons Fish stock (opposite)*
pinch of saffron	*pinch of saffron*
7.5 ml/1½ teaspoons olive oil	*1½ teaspoons olive oil*
7.5 ml/1½ teaspoons shallot vinegar	*1½ teaspoons shallot vinegar*
juice of 1 small lime	*juice of 1 small lime*
salt and pepper	*salt and pepper*

To serve

75 g/3 oz dried edible seaweed	*3 oz dried edible seaweed*
8 oysters on half shell	*8 oysters on half shell*
8 cooked Mediterranean prawns, tails removed	*8 jumbo shrimp, cooked, tails removed*
sprigs of chervil	*sprigs of chervil*

Sauce

50 ml/2 fl oz Tomato coulis (page 72)	*¼ cup Tomato coulis (page 72)*
1 teaspoon horseradish sauce	*½ teaspoon grated horseradish mixed with 1 teaspoon sour cream*
1 drop Tabasco	*1 drop Tabasco*
1 drop Worcestershire sauce	*1 drop Worcestershire sauce*

Serves 4

Preparation time: 50 minutes

Cooking time: 10 minutes

Marinating time: 12 hours

1 Place the Atlantic seaweed, if available, in the pan of a double steamer containing 900 ml/1½ pints of cold water.

2 Scrub the mussels very well in plenty of cold water and place in the steamer basket. Set aside until the water in the base of steamer has come to the boil, then set the basket of mussels on top.

3 Cover and steam for about 4 minutes until the mussels are all open. Discard any that do not open. Remove the mussels and discard the shells.

4 Heat the fish stock to simmering in a saucepan. Infuse the saffron for 30 seconds. Remove from the heat and leave the liquid to cool in a bowl.

5 Add the olive oil, shallot vinegar, lime juice, and salt and pepper to the cooled fish stock.

6 Add the cooked, shelled mussels to the marinade, cover and leave in the refrigerator for 12 hours.

7 Soak the edible seaweed in cold water for 30 minutes. Drain through a fine sieve, pressing out the water, and set aside.

8 To make the sauce, mix the Tomato coulis, horseradish sauce (grated horseradish and sour cream), Tabasco and Worcestershire sauce in a glass bowl. Mix well, season to taste and refrigerate until serving time. Place in a serving bowl.

9 Strain the marinade into a bowl and set aside.

10 The mussels and oysters should be served in individual small scallop shells, on each plate. Place a little edible seaweed on each plate. Arrange 2 prawns as a centrepiece. Put a scallop shell of mussels and a scallop shell of prawns on each plate. Spoon a little marinade into each shell. Garnish with a sprig of chervil. Pass the sauce separately.

Oysters, Mediterranean Prawns (Shrimp), and Marinated Mussels with a Spiced Cocktail Sauce
Breast of Duck with Pineapple and Rose (Pink) Peppercorns

Fish Stock

METRIC/IMPERIAL

25 g/1 oz butter or margarine
100 g/4 oz onions, peeled and sliced
1 kg/2 lb white fish bones (preferably
sole, whiting, turbot, etc), viscera
and gills removed
1 bay leaf
juice of ½ small lemon
parsley stalks
3 peppercorns
2.25 litres/4 pints water

AMERICAN

2 tablespoons butter or margarine
1 medium onion, peeled and sliced
2 lb white fish bones from any non-
oily fish (flounder, sole, whiting,
weakfish), viscera and gills removed
1 bay leaf
juice of ½ a small lemon
parsley stalks
3 peppercorns
5 pints water

Makes 1.75 litres/
3 pints/3¾ pints (US)

Preparation time:
10 minutes

Cooking time:
30 minutes

1 Melt the butter or margarine in a very large heavy-based pan. Add the onions, fish bones and all the other ingredients except the water. Cover the pan with greaseproof (waxed) paper and a lid and cook gently for 5 minutes.
2 Remove the paper and add the water. Bring to the boil, skim and simmer for 20 minutes only. Strain and cool.
3 Chill in the refrigerator, where it will keep for 2-3 days. Fish stock can be frozen for up to 1 month.

71

Tomato Coulis

METRIC/IMPERIAL	AMERICAN
25 g/1 oz butter	2 tablespoons butter
¼ medium onion, chopped	1 small onion, chopped
3 basil leaves, chopped	3 basil leaves, chopped
10 tomatoes, roughly chopped	10 tomatoes, roughly chopped
few drops of Tabasco	few drops of Tabasco
1 x 2.5 ml spoon/½ teaspoon Worcestershire sauce	½ teaspoon Worcestershire sauce
salt and pepper	salt and pepper

Makes 600 ml/ 1 pint/1¼ pints (US)

1 Melt the butter in a pan, add the onion and chopped basil and cook gently for a few minutes.
2 Add the tomatoes, cover the pan and cook for about 15 minutes until very soft.
3 Pour the mixture into a liquidizer, add the sauces and blend well. Season.
4 Strain the sauce through a fine sieve to remove all skin and seeds. Leave to cool.

Breast of Duck with Pineapple and Rose (Pink) Peppercorns

METRIC/IMPERIAL	AMERICAN
4 boneless duck breasts	4 boneless duck breasts
salt and pepper	salt and pepper
40 g/1½ oz butter	3 tablespoons butter
½ small pineapple, cut into 20 thin slices	½ small pineapple, cut into 20 thin slices

Sauce

METRIC/IMPERIAL	AMERICAN
900 ml/1½ pints Duck stock (page 117)	3¾ cups Duck stock (page 117)
15 g/½ oz butter	1 tablespoon butter
1 x 5 ml spoon/1 teaspoon chopped shallots	1 teaspoon chopped shallots
85 ml/3 fl oz pineapple juice	6 tablespoons pineapple juice
1 x 5 ml spoon/1 teaspoon white wine vinegar	1 teaspoon white wine vinegar
1 x 2.5 ml spoon/½ teaspoon rose peppercorns, crushed	½ teaspoon pink peppercorns, crushed
1 x 1.25 ml spoon/¼ teaspoon raw ginger, peeled and chopped	¼ teaspoon raw ginger, peeled and chopped
85 ml/3 fl oz port	6 tablespoons port

To garnish

METRIC/IMPERIAL	AMERICAN
4 wild mushrooms (chanterelles)	4 wild mushrooms (chanterelles)
1 x 5 ml spoon/1 teaspoon rose peppercorns	1 teaspoon pink peppercorns
4 spring onions, cut into brushes	4 scallions, cut into brushes

Serves 4

Preparation time: 30-45 minutes

Cooking time: 7-8 minutes

Oven: 190°C, 375°F, Gas Mark 5

1 To make the sauce, pour the duck stock into a heavy-based pan and reduce to 300 ml/½ pint/1¼ cups.
2 Meanwhile, melt the butter and cook the shallots for 1 minute. Add the pineapple juice, vinegar, peppercorns, ginger and port and reduce the liquor by half.
3 Add the duck stock and reduce again by one-third. Season to taste and keep hot.
4 Season the duck breasts. Melt the butter in a frying pan, place the duck breasts skin side down and fry until golden brown. Turn and brown the other side.
5 Place the duck breasts on a rack in a roasting tin and cook in a preheated oven for about 7-8 minutes. (The breasts are served very pink.) Remove from the oven and allow to cool slightly.
6 For each serving, place 5 slices of pineapple on a plate. Slice the duck and arrange in a fan shape, covering half the pineapple. Place a mushroom, open side up, in the centre and fill the cavity with a few rose (pink) peppercorns.
7 Strain the sauce and pour a little on to each plate. Garnish with a spring onion (scallion) brush.

Brandy Snap Baskets with Raspberry Sorbet and Berries

METRIC/IMPERIAL	AMERICAN
40 g/1½ oz butter	3 tablespoons butter
1 tablespoon golden syrup	1 tablespoon light corn syrup (or half light and half dark)
10 g/2 level teaspoons ground ginger	2 level teaspoons powdered ginger
20 g/1½ tablespoons plain flour	1½ tablespoons all-purpose flour
175 g/6 oz blueberries	1 cup blueberries

Raspberry sorbet

METRIC/IMPERIAL	AMERICAN
175 ml/6 fl oz Raspberry coulis (below)	¾ cup Raspberry coulis (below)
175 ml/6 fl oz Stock syrup (page 95)	¾ cup Stock syrup (page 95)
1 egg white, lightly beaten	1 egg white, lightly beaten

To serve

METRIC/IMPERIAL	AMERICAN
Raspberry coulis (below)	Raspberry coulis (below)
4 mint leaves	4 mint leaves

Serves 4

Preparation time: 20 minutes

Cooking time: 10-15 minutes

Freezing time: 30 minutes

Oven: 230°C, 450°F, Gas Mark 8

1 Melt the butter in a heavy-based pan. Over a low heat, mix in the golden (corn) syrup, ginger and flour until a smooth consistency is reached.

2 Grease a baking (cookie) sheet and drop 4 teaspoons of the mixture, spaced well apart. (The rounds of mixture will expand to approximately 7.5 cm/3 inches in diameter.) Bake in a preheated oven for 10-15 minutes, taking care that they do not over-brown.

3 Remove from the oven and allow to cool slightly. Place each round in a teacup, pressing firmly into the base to form the contour. Leave to cool then remove from the cups.

4 Prepare the sorbet: mix the raspberry coulis and stock syrup together and pour into an ice-cream or sorbet maker and freeze to a slush (following the manufacturer's instructions). When the sorbet is slushy, turn into a bowl and add the lightly beaten egg white. Freeze for about 30 minutes.

5 Pour a coating of Raspberry coulis on to each dessert plate and sprinkle blueberries on top of the sauce. Place the brandy snap basket in the centre of the plate and fill with raspberry sorbet. Decorate each with a mint leaf.

Raspberry Coulis

METRIC/IMPERIAL	AMERICAN
50 ml/ 2 fl oz water	¼ cup water
450 g/1 lb fresh or frozen raspberries	1 lb fresh or frozen raspberries
75 g/3 oz caster sugar	6 tablespoons (⅜ cup) superfine or granulated sugar

Makes 300 ml/ ½ pint/1¼ cups

Preparation time: 30 minutes

1 Bring the water to the boil in a heavy-based pan, add the raspberries and sugar and simmer until very soft.

2 Press the mixture through a conical strainer, transfer to a jam (jelly) bag and leave suspended over a basin until all the juice has drained through. The bag must be supported so that the bottom of it does not dip into the juice in the basin.

3 Pour the clear juice into a small bowl, cover and refrigerate until ready to serve.

Smoked Salmon and Slices of Pear filled with Cottage Cheese and Chives

Beef, Veal and Lamb Fondue with Chutney, Plum and Mint Dips

Chocolate Mousse flavoured with Rum

Smoked Salmon and Slices of Pear filled with Cottage Cheese and Chives

METRIC/IMPERIAL	AMERICAN
600 ml/1 pint cold water	*1¼ pints (2½ cups) cold water*
juice of 1 lemon	*juice of 1 lemon*
6 mint sprigs	*6 mint sprigs*
50 g/2 oz caster sugar	*4 tablespoons superfine sugar*
1 cinnamon stick	*1 cinnamon stick*
2 whole pears, peeled	*2 whole pears, peeled*
4 dessertspoons cottage cheese	*3 tablespoons cottage cheese*
1 dessertspoon chopped chives	*2 teaspoons chopped chives*
pinch of paprika pepper	*pinch of paprika pepper*
8 slices smoked salmon	*8 slices smoked salmon*
4 leaves red frizzy lettuce, to garnish	*4 leaves red-leaf or red-edged curly lettuce, to garnish*

Serves 4

Preparation time: 15 minutes

Cooking time: about 13 minutes

Cooling time: 1 hour

1 Pour the cold water into a pan wide enough to contain the pears lying on their sides. Add the lemon juice, mint, sugar and cinnamon stick.

2 Place the pears in the liquid and heat until simmering. The liquid must cover the pears completely. Poach for 5-10 minutes, remove from the heat and leave the pears to cool in the syrup for about 1 hour.

3 Using an apple corer, remove the centres from the pears.

4 Mix the cottage cheese, chives and paprika pepper and fill the pear cavities with the mixture. Cut each pear horizontally into 6 slices.

5 For each portion, place 2 slices of smoked salmon on one side of the plate, and arrange 3 pear slices so that they slightly overlap the salmon. Garnish each plate with the red-edged lettuce.

Beef, Veal and Lamb Fondue with Chutney, Plum and Mint Dips

	METRIC/IMPERIAL	AMERICAN
Mint dip	2 x 150 ml/5 fl oz cartons natural yogurt	*1¼ cups plain unflavored yogurt*
	12 leaves fresh mint, chopped	*12 leaves fresh mint, chopped*
	juice of ½ lime	*juice of ½ lime*
	1 x 15 ml/1 tablespoon chopped parsley	*1 tablespoon chopped parsley*
	salt and pepper	*salt and pepper*
Chutney dip	450 g/1 lb hard mangoes, peeled and stoned	*1 lb hard mangoes, peeled and stoned*
	100 g/4 oz chopped sultanas	*¾ cup white raisins*
	50 g/2 oz chopped cashew nuts	*½ cup chopped cashews*
	25 g/1 oz chopped fresh ginger	*1 inch piece fresh ginger, peeled and chopped*
	1 garlic clove	*1 garlic clove*
	1 chilli pepper, seeded and chopped	*1 small hot pepper, seeded and chopped*
	225 g/8 oz brown sugar	*1½ cups dark brown sugar*
	200 ml/1/3 pint cider vinegar	*scant cup (7 fl oz) cider vinegar*

*In The Equestrian Centre: Smoked Salmon and Slices of Pear filled with Cottage Cheese and Chives
Beef, Veal and Lamb Fondue with Chutney, Plum and Mint Dips*

Plum dip

25 g/1 oz butter	*2 tablespoons butter*
8 ripe plums, stoned	*8 ripe plums, stoned*
100 g/4 oz caster sugar	*½ cup superfine or granulated sugar*
juice of 1 lemon	*juice of 1 lemon*
1 x 2.5 ml spoon/½ teaspoon ground cinnamon	*½ teaspoon ground cinnamon*
25 g/1 oz fresh ginger, chopped	*1 inch piece fresh ginger, peeled and chopped*
2 dessertspoons cold water	*3 teaspoons cold water*

350 g/12 oz lean sirloin of beef, cut into 12 cubes	¾ lb lean sirloin of beef, cut into 12 cubes
350 g/12 oz lean loin of veal, cut into 12 cubes	¾ lb lean loin of veal, cut into 12 cubes
350 g/12 oz lean loin of lamb, cut into 12 cubes	¾ lb lean loin of lamb, cut into 12 cubes
36 thin slices of cucumber	36 thin slices cucumber
12 radishes, cut into 'flowers'	12 radishes, cut into 'flowers'
cress	handful of watercress, washed
900 ml/1½ pints corn oil, for cooking	2 pints corn oil, for cooking

Serves 4

**Preparation time:
30 minutes**

**Cooking time:
30 minutes**

1 To prepare the mint dip, combine all the ingredients, mix well and leave to stand for 1 hour. Taste and add more seasoning if needed.

2 To make the chutney dip, place all the ingredients in a heavy based pan and bring to the boil. Lower the heat and simmer for 30 minutes, stirring occasionally to make sure the chutney is not sticking to the pan. Cool.

3 To prepare the plum dip, melt the butter in a heavy based pan, add all the ingredients and stir to combine. Bring to the boil, lower the heat and simmer for 15 minutes, stirring occasionally. Liquidize or blend in a food processor and set aside to cool.

4 Place each sauce in a decorative serving bowl.

5 For each portion, arrange 9 cucumber slices in 3 sections. In one section, place 3 cubes of beef, in another 3 cubes of veal, and in the third section 3 cubes of lamb. Decorate each plate with 3 radish flowers and some cress (watercress leaves).

6 Heat the oil in a fondue pot at the table, to frying temperature. Each person cooks his or her own meat – holding each cube on a fondue skewer for about 1 – 1¼ minutes before removing and dipping into one or more of the sauces.

Chocolate Mousse flavoured with Rum

METRIC/IMPERIAL	AMERICAN
90 g/3½ oz dark plain dessert chocolate (Bournville), broken into pieces	3½ squares semi-sweet chocolate broken into pieces
3 eggs, size 3, separated	3 medium eggs, separated
40 g/1½ oz caster sugar	3 tablespoons superfine sugar
100 ml/1½ fl oz double cream, whipped	½ cup (3½ fl oz) heavy cream, whipped
40 ml/1½ fl oz dark rum	3 tablespoons dark rum

Serves 4

**Preparation time:
10 minutes**

**Chilling time:
2 hours**

1 Melt the chocolate in a bowl over a pan of hot water.

2 In another bowl, mix the egg yolks with half the sugar and beat until light and fluffy.

3 In a third bowl, whisk the egg whites with the remaining sugar until they stand in stiff, glossy peaks.

4 With the bowl of melted chocolate set over hot water, fold in the egg yolk and sugar mixture and mix thoroughly. Remove from the heat and stir in the rum. Gently fold in the meringue, then the whipped cream and mix in lightly.

5 Spoon or pipe into glasses and leave to set in the refrigerator for at least 2 hours.

Carrot and Orange Soup   Stilton and Red Wine Pâté

Venison Pâté with Blackcurrant Sauce

Wholemeal Loaves with Ham and Pineapple, Cream Cheese and Grapes

Vegetable and Leek Broth

Carrot and Orange Soup

METRIC/IMPERIAL	AMERICAN
100 g/4 oz butter	½ cup butter
350 g/12 oz carrots, peeled and roughly chopped	¾ lb carrots, peeled and roughly chopped
3 sticks celery, trimmed and roughly chopped	3 sticks celery, trimmed and roughly chopped
1 small onion, peeled and roughly chopped	1 small onion, peeled and roughly chopped
1 small leek (white part only), well washed and roughly chopped	1 small leek (white part only), well washed and roughly chopped
1 small orange, peeled and roughly chopped	1 small orange, peeled and roughly chopped
1 litre/1¾ pints Chicken stock (page 51)	2¼ pints Chicken stock (page 51)
2 medium potatoes, peeled and roughly chopped	2 medium potatoes, peeled and roughly chopped
salt and pepper	salt and pepper
50-60 ml/2-2½ fl oz double cream	¼ cup heavy cream
2 thick slices white bread, crusts removed and cut into 5 mm/¼ inch dice	2 thick slices white bread, crusts removed and cut into ¼ inch dice
chopped parsley	chopped parsley

Serves 4

Preparation time: 15 minutes

Cooking time: 50-55 minutes

1 Melt 75 g/3 oz of the butter in a heavy-based pan. Add the carrots, celery, onions and leek and cook for a few minutes, without colouring, stirring constantly.

2 Add the orange and the stock and bring to the boil. Add the potatoes and simmer for approximately 45 minutes until the vegetables are tender.

3 Pour the soup into a blender or food processor (you may have to do this in 2 batches), purée, then strain through a fine sieve into a clean saucepan. Season and stir in the double cream.

4 In a large frying pan, melt the remaining butter and when hot but not brown, fry the bread cubes until golden brown, stirring constantly.

5 Just before serving, add the chopped parsley to the soup. Pour into individual bowls and sprinkle with croûtons.

Stilton and Red Wine Pâté   Wholemeal Loaves with Ham and Pineapple, Cream Cheese and Grapes   Vegetable and Leek Broth

Stilton and Red Wine Pâté

METRIC/IMPERIAL

100 g/4 oz Stilton
50 ml/2 fl oz light cream
50 ml/2 fl oz double cream
2 fl oz red wine
½ level teaspoon powdered
gelatine, or ½ leaf gelatine

AMERICAN

¼ lb Stilton
¼ cup light cream
¼ cup heavy cream
4 tablespoons red wine
1 level teaspoon gelatin

Serves 6

**Preparation time:
10 minutes**

**Chilling time:
1 hour**

1 Mash the Stilton with a fork until it is creamy and smooth. Add the single (light) cream and beat again, then mix in the double (heavy) cream and beat until smooth.
2 Place the mixture in a piping (pastry) bag with a 5 mm/¼ inch plain nozzle and pipe into 6 individual ramekin dishes. Chill.
3 If using leaf gelatine, soak it in water according to the instructions on the packet. Then heat the red wine in a saucepan and stir in the gelatine and dissolve.
4 Spoon 2 tablespoons of the red wine mixture over each dish of pâté and leave to set in the refrigerator. (If any of the red wine aspic is left over, divide it equally between the dishes before chilling.)

Venison Pâté with Blackcurrant Sauce

	METRIC/IMPERIAL	AMERICAN
	75 g/3 oz butter	6 tablespoons butter
	1 onion, peeled and chopped	1 onion, peeled and chopped
	350 g/12 oz lean venison, coarsely minced	¾ lb lean venison meat, coarsley ground
	1 garlic clove, peeled and chopped	1 garlic clove, peeled and chopped
	salt and pepper	salt and pepper
	175 g/6 oz lean pork, finely minced	¾ cup pork, finely ground
	150 ml/¼ pint red wine	generous ½ cup (5 fl oz) red wine
	50 g/2 oz toasted pine-nut kernels	⅓ cup toasted pine-nut kernels
Blackcurrant sauce	225 g/8 oz blackcurrants	½ lb blackcurrants, if available, or unsweetened frozen blackberries*
	50 g/2 oz caster sugar	4 tablespoons superfine or granulated sugar
	2 dessertspoons warm water	2 tablespoons warm water
Port jelly	85 ml/3 fl oz water	scant ½ cup water
	2 x 5 ml spoons/2 teaspoons powdered gelatine	2 teaspoons gelatin powder
	50 ml/2 fl oz port	¼ cup port

*If using American blackberries, adjust the amount of sugar when the berries are almost cooked. Press through a sieve to remove seeds.

Serves 8

Preparation time: 15 minutes

Resting time: overnight

Cooking time: 70 minutes

Oven: 180°C, 350°F, Gas Mark 4

1 Melt the butter, add the onion and fry for 2 minutes.

2 Mix with the venison. Add the garlic, salt and pepper, pork and red wine. Mix well, put in a refrigerator container or bowl, cover and leave to stand overnight in the refrigerator.

3 Remove, mix thoroughly again and add the toasted pine nut kernels.

4 Transfer the mixture to a 20 x 10 x 9 cm/8 x 4 x 3½ inch terrine and cook in a pre-heated oven for 1 hour.

5 While the pâté is cooking, prepare the blackcurrant sauce: place all the ingredients together in a saucepan and cook gently for about 10 minutes, until the mixture is the consistency of thin jam. Cool and store in a screw top jar in the refrigerator until needed.

6 To prepare the port jelly, bring the water to the boil and add the gelatine. Remove from the heat. When the gelatine is dissolved, add the port.

7 To test if the pâté is cooked, push a skewer into the centre: if it comes out clean the pâté is cooked. Remove from the oven and pour in the port jelly. Leave to cool completely.

8 Serve 1 dessertspoon blackcurrant sauce with each portion of pâté.

Wholemeal Loaves with Ham, Pineapple, Cream Cheese and Grapes

	METRIC/IMPERIAL	AMERICAN
	8 individual wholemeal loaves	8 miniature wholewheat loaves
	8 sprigs red frizzy lettuce	8 sprigs red-edged lettuce or radicchio
Ham and pineapple	175 g/6 oz cooked ham, cut into 5 mm/¼ inch dice	¾ cup cooked ham, cut into ¼ inch dice
	175 g/6 oz fresh pineapple, cut into 5 mm/¼ inch dice	¾ cup fresh pineapple, cut into ¼ inch dice
	2 x 5 ml spoons/2 teaspoons chopped chives	2 teaspoons chopped chives

Cream cheese	100 g/4 oz full fat cream cheese	*½ cup (4 oz) cream cheese*
and grapes	12 black grapes, halved and seeded	*12 black grapes, halved and seeded*
	juice of 1 lemon	*juice of 1 lemon*
	pinch of paprika	*pinch of paprika*

Makes 8 individual loaves

Preparation time: 20 minutes

1 Cut the tops off the mini-loaves and scoop out the centre with a spoon, leaving the shell intact.

2 Put a sprig of red lettuce inside each loaf at the one end.

3 Mix together the diced ham and pineapple. Stir in the chopped chives and fill 4 of the loaves with this mixture.

4 Cream the cheese until very soft. Add the grapes, lemon juice and paprika and mix well. Spoon into the remaining 4 loaves.

Vegetable and Leek Broth

METRIC/IMPERIAL	AMERICAN
40 g/1½ oz butter	*3 tablespoons butter*
50 g/2 oz onions, peeled and finely chopped	*scant ½ cup onions, peeled and finely chopped*
50 g/2 oz carrots, peeled and grated	*scant ½ cup carrots, peeled and grated*
50 g/2 oz turnips, peeled and grated	*scant ½ cup turnips, peeled and grated*
175 g/6 oz leeks, trimmed and diced	*1 cup leeks, trimmed and diced*
1.2 litres/2 pints strong Chicken stock (page 51)	*2½ pints (5 cups) strong Chicken stock (page 51)*
good pinch of chopped thyme	*good pinch of chopped thyme*
1 small bay leaf	*1 small bay leaf*
100 g/4 oz potatoes, peeled and diced	*1 medium potato (about ¼ lb), peeled and diced*
salt and pepper	*salt and pepper*
1 x 5 ml spoon/1 rounded teaspoon chopped parsley, to garnish	*1 rounded teaspoon chopped parsley, to garnish*

Serves 4

Preparation time: 10 minutes

Cooking time: about 1 hour

1 Melt the butter in a large pan. Add the onions, carrots, turnips and leeks and cook, without colouring, for 5 minutes.

2 Add the stock to the pan and stir in the thyme and bay leaf. Bring to the boil, reduce the heat and simmer for 30 minutes.

3 Add the potatoes and cook for a further 10 minutes. Remove the bay leaf.

4 Correct the seasoning. Serve in warmed bowls, garnishing each one with chopped parsley.

Saffron Marinated Scallops with Mustard Sauce

METRIC/IMPERIAL	AMERICAN
8 King (very large) scallops, shelled and cleaned	*8 large sea scallops, shelled and cleaned*
40 ml/3 tablespoons olive oil	*2 tablespoons olive oil*
1 x 2.5 ml spoon/½ teaspoon saffron	*½ teaspoon saffron*
juice of 1 small lime	*juice of 1 small lime*
1½ shallots, peeled and finely chopped	*1½ shallots, peeled and finely chopped*
65 ml/2½ fl oz (5 tablespoons) dry white wine	*5 tablespoons dry white wine*
20 ml/1 tablespoon plus 15 ml/1 teaspoon shallot vinegar	*1 tablespoon plus 1 teaspoon shallot vinegar*
1 rounded dessertspoon Scottish wholegrain mustard	*1 rounded teaspoon wholegrain mustard*
salt and pepper	*salt and pepper*

To garnish

2 bunches watercress	*2 bunches watercress*
50 g/2 oz Keta (red) caviar	*2 oz red salmon caviar*

Serves 4

Preparation time: 10 minutes

Cooking time: 5-8 minutes

Marinating time: 24 hours

1 Cut each scallop horizontally into 4 slices and arrange in a shallow glass or earthenware pan. Sprinkle with salt and pepper.

2 Put the olive oil, saffron, lime juice, shallots, white wine and vinegar into a pan. Bring the mixture to the boil and cook until the saffron has infused and the mixture is golden brown.

3 Pour the hot liquid over the scallops. Press the scallops with the back of a spoon to make sure they are totally submerged in the liquid.

4 Cover with cling film (saran wrap) and refrigerate for 24 hours.

5 Remove the scallops with a slotted spoon and strain the marinade into a bowl.

6 To make the mustard dressing, whisk the wholegrain mustard into the strained marinade. Season to taste.

7 Arrange half a bunch of watercress in a curve around the edges of a dinner plate. Arrange 8 scallop slices in the centre and spoon over 2 dessertspoons (2 heaped teaspoons) of mustard dressing. Divide the red caviar into 4 portions, and spoon it on top of the scallops just before serving.

Pastry Pouch of Lamb, Calf's Liver and Herbs with Port Sauce

METRIC/IMPERIAL	AMERICAN
225 g/8 oz lamb loin (eye only), cut into 25 g/1 oz pieces	*½ lb lamb loin (eye only), cut into 1 oz pieces*
225 g/8 oz calf's liver, cut into 25 g/1 oz pieces	*½ lb calf's liver, cut into 1 oz pieces*
salt and pepper	*salt and pepper*
40 g/1½ oz butter	*2½ tablespoons butter*
16 squares filo pastry (about 25 cm/10 inches square)	*16 squares filo pastry (about 10 inches square)*
melted butter, for brushing	*melted butter, for brushing*
4 sprigs rosemary	*4 sprigs rosemary*

	METRIC/IMPERIAL	AMERICAN
Chicken and herb mousse	100 g/4 oz uncooked white chicken meat, skin and bone removed 250 ml/8 fl oz double cream salt and freshly ground white pepper 1 x 2.5 ml spoon/½ teaspoon fresh chopped rosemary 1 x 2.5 ml spoon/½ teaspoon fresh chopped thyme	4 oz uncooked white chicken meat, skin and bone removed 1 cup heavy cream salt and freshly ground white pepper ½ teaspoon fresh chopped rosemary ½ teaspoon fresh chopped thyme
Port sauce	175 ml/7 fl oz Veal glaze (below) 50 ml/12 fl oz ruby port 1 sprig rosemary	⅞ cup Veal glaze (below) ¼ cup ruby port 1 sprig rosemary

Serves 4

Preparation time: 25 minutes

Chilling time: 2 hours

Cooking time: 20-25 minutes

Oven: 180°C, 350°F, Gas Mark 4

1 To make the chicken and herb mousse, place the chicken meat in a blender or food processor and blend until smooth. Run the purée through a fine sieve. Place in a bowl over ice and add the cream a little at a time, mixing vigorously until a light mousse is produced. Season and add the herbs.

2 Season the lamb and calf's liver.

3 Melt the butter in a shallow frying pan and heat until hot but not brown. Flash fry the lamb and liver separately until sealed on all sides. Leave to cool. Slice each piece of cooked meat in half.

4 Lay out 8 double-thick layers of filo pastry squares. Place 1 dessertspoon (1 heaped teaspoon) of chicken and herb mousse in the centre and press down until about 5 mm/¼ inch thick and about 5 cm/2 inches round.

5 Place 2 pieces of lamb and 2 pieces of liver in alternate layers on top of the mousse. Lightly brush the filo pastry borders with melted butter. Gather the 4 corners of a pastry square, bringing them up to the centre over the meat. Pinch the pastry together at the neck of the pouch. Repeat for the remaining squares and transfer to a greased baking (cookie) sheet. Brush carefully with melted butter and refrigerate for 2 hours.

6 Place the pouches in a preheated oven and bake for 15-20 minutes or until crisp and golden.

7 While the pouches bake, make the port sauce: place all the ingredients in a heavy-based pan, bring to the boil and reduce by one-third. Adjust the seasoning and strain.

8 Carefully cut each pastry pouch in half from top to bottom. Pour a little sauce on to each plate and place 2 pouches on top, leaving a gap between the halves so that the inner layers can be seen. Repeat for all portions. Garnish each with a sprig of rosemary.

Veal Glaze

	METRIC/IMPERIAL	AMERICAN
	2.25 litres/2 pints Veal stock (page 117) ½ onion, peeled and chopped 6 mushrooms, roughly chopped few parsley stalks 150 ml/¼ pint dry red wine	2½ pints Veal stock (page 117) ½ onion, peeled and chopped 6 mushrooms, roughly chopped few parsley stalks generous ½ cup (5 fl oz) dry red wine

Makes about 475 ml/ 16-17 fl oz/1 pint (US)

1 Pour the stock into a heavy-based pan, bring to the boil and reduce to 600 ml/ 1 pint/1¼ pints.

2 Add the onion, mushrooms, parsley and wine and reduce by one-third.

Preparation time: 5 minutes   Cooking time: about 2 hours

Sliced Fresh Fruit with Melted Chocolate

METRIC/IMPERIAL

2 kiwi fruits, peeled
1 orange, peeled and
segmented
½ galia melon, peeled
12 strawberries, hulled
20 blackberries
350 g/12 oz dark plain
dessert chocolate, broken into
pieces
2 dessertspoons double cream

AMERICAN

2 kiwi fruits, peeled
1 orange, peeled and
segmented
½ galia or honeydew melon, peeled
12 strawberries, hulled
20 blackberries
12 squares (¾ lb) semi-
sweet chocolate, broken into
pieces
3 teaspoons heavy cream

Serves 4

**Preparation time:
15 minutes**

**Cooking time:
about 10 minutes**

1 Cut the fruits into fairly large pieces and arrange on 4 plates in a decorative pattern.

2 Melt the chocolate in a bowl over hot water. Pour into a hot, dry serving bowl and keep warm.

3 Just before serving, pour the double (heavy) cream into the chocolate and swirl to make a pretty pattern (do not mix). Serve at once so that the chocolate remains hot and liquid for dipping the fruits.

Sliced Fresh Fruit with Melted Chocolate

AUTUMN PICNIC

Country Pâté

Roast Chicken

Veal and Ham Pie

Anchovy Bread

Olive and Onion Bread

Roast Sirloin of Beef

Country Pâté

METRIC/IMPERIAL	AMERICAN
450 g/1 lb chicken livers, trimmed	*1 lb chicken livers, trimmed*
150 g/5 oz pork fat	*1 cup pork fat (fatback)*
150 g/5 oz veal trimmings	*1 scant cup veal (stewing veal or trimmings from a veal roast)*
150 g/5 oz belly pork	*1 scant cup boneless fresh pork sparerib*
70 ml/2½ fl oz/3 tablespoons brandy	*3 tablespoons brandy*
70 ml/2½ fl oz/3 tablespoons sherry	*3 tablespoons sherry*
1 x 2.5 ml spoon/½ teaspoon chopped thyme	*½ teaspoon chopped thyme*
1 x 2.5 ml spoon/½ teaspoon saltpetre	*½ teaspoon saltpetre (available from pharmacies)*
1 garlic clove, peeled and chopped	*1 garlic clove, peeled and chopped*
salt and pepper	*salt and pepper*
1 egg, size 1, beaten	*1 jumbo egg, beaten*
50 ml/2 fl oz double cream	*¼ cup heavy cream*
6 rashers bacon	*6 strips bacon*

Port jelly

85 ml/3 fl oz water	*scant ½ cup water*
2 x 5 ml spoons/2 teaspoons powdered gelatine	*2 teaspoons gelatin powder*
50 ml/2 fl oz port	*¼ cup port*

Serves 10

Preparation time: 20 minutes

Resting time: overnight

Cooking time: about 1 hour

Oven: 230°C, 450°F, Gas Mark 8, then: 190°C, 375°F, Gas Mark 5

1 Coarsely mince the livers, pork fat (fatback), veal, belly pork (boneless pork spareribs) and put in a bowl.

2 Add the brandy, sherry, thyme, saltpetre, garlic, salt and pepper and mix well. Place in a container with a tight lid, cover and leave to marinate overnight in a refrigerator.

3 Place the mixture in a food processor or blender (divided into several batches) and blend to a purée. Add the egg and double (heavy) cream and correct the seasoning. Mix well. Preheat the oven to the higher temperature.

4 Line a 20 x 10 x 9 cm/8 x 4 x 3½ inch terrine or mould with the bacon. Pour in the pâté mixture.

5 Cover with foil or a lid and set in a bain marie (roasting tin half-filled with hot water). Cook in a preheated oven for 15 minutes. Reduce the heat and cook for a further 45 minutes.

6 While the pâté is cooking, prepare the port jelly. Bring the water to the boil and add the gelatine. Remove from the heat. When the gelatine has completely dissolved, add the port.

7 Remove the pâté from the oven and pour in the port jelly. Leave to cool.

Roast Chicken

METRIC/IMPERIAL	AMERICAN
1 x 1.25 kg/2½ lb chicken	*1 x 2½ lb chicken*
salt and pepper	*salt and pepper*
50 g/2 oz sunflower, safflower or	*4 tablespoons sunflower, safflower or*
soya margarine	*soy margarine*

Serves 4-6

Preparation time: 5 minutes

1 Wash and dry the chicken inside and out and season with salt and pepper.
2 Melt the margarine in a heavy frying pan and seal the chicken on all sides.
3 Roast on a rack over a tray in a preheated oven, basting occasionally, for 1 hour 10 minutes, or until the juices run clear when a skewer is inserted into the thigh (second joint). Leave to cool completely.

Cooking time: 1 hour 10 minutes   Oven:230°C, 450°F, Gas Mark 8

Veal and Ham Pie

METRIC/IMPERIAL	AMERICAN
750 g/1½ lb lean veal, minced	*1½ lb lean veal, minced*
50 g/2 oz uncooked gammon, minced	*¼ cup ham, minced*
1 x 15 ml spoon/1 tablespoon chopped parsley	*1 tablespoon chopped parsley*
1 x 15 ml spoon/1 tablespoon chopped thyme	*1 tablespoon chopped fresh thyme*
salt and black pepper	*salt and black pepper*
grated zest of 1 lemon	*grated zest of 1 lemon*
3 eggs, size 1, hard-boiled and shelled	*3 jumbo eggs, hard-cooked and shelled*

Hot water paste

150 ml/¼ pint water	*½ cup plus 2 tablespoons water*
50 g/2 oz lard	*4 tablespoons lard*
salt	*salt*
225 g/8 oz plain flour	*2 cups all-purpose flour*
beaten egg, for brushing	*beaten egg, for brushing*

Port jelly

85 ml/3 fl oz water	*scant ½ cup water*
2 x 5 ml spoons/2 teaspoons powdered gelatine	*2 teaspoons gelatin powder*
50 ml/2 fl oz port	*¼ cup port*

Makes a 1 kg/ 2 lb loaf

Preparation time: 30 minutes

Cooking time: about 2 hours 15 minutes

Setting time: overnight

Oven: 230°C, 450°F, Gas Mark 8 then: 150°C, 300°F, Gas Mark 2

1 To prepare the hot water paste, place the water, lard and salt in a pan and bring to the boil. Sift the flour into a bowl.
2 Pour the boiling mixture on to the flour and mix to form a dough. Roll out on a lightly floured board. Cut out a rectangle large enough to line a 1 kg/2 lb loaf tin. Re-roll the trimmings to a rectangle to form a lid.
3 Line the tin, bringing the pastry slightly over the edges.
4 Mix the veal and gammon (ham) and add the parsley, thyme, salt and pepper and lemon zest. Mix thoroughly.
5 Spoon a layer of this mixture, approximately 5 mm/¼ inch deep, in the bottom of the lined loaf tin. Place the eggs lengthways down the centre of the tin.
6 Cover with the remaining meat mixture, then place the pastry lid on top. Crimp the edges together. Make leaf shapes of any remaining pastry and use to decorate the lid. Cut 2 holes, approximately 5 mm/¼ inch in diameter, in the top of the pastry, to allow steam to escape during cooking.
7 Brush the top of the pastry with beaten egg, then place the pie in a preheated oven and cook for 15 minutes. Reduce the oven temperature and continue to cook for a further 1½-2 hours.
8 While the pie is cooking, prepare the port jelly. Bring the water to the boil and add the gelatine. Remove from the heat. When the gelatine has completely dissolved, add the port.
9 Remove the pie from the oven and pour the port jelly through the holes in the pastry lid. Allow to cool completely, then leave in the refrigerator to set overnight.

Anchovy Bread

METRIC/IMPERIAL	AMERICAN
6 x 15 ml spoons/6 tablespoons warm water	6 tablespoons warm water
450 ml/¾ pint warm milk	15 fl oz warm milk
25 g/1 oz fresh yeast*	1 oz fresh yeast*
40 g/1½ oz brown sugar	¼ cup firmly packed light brown sugar
225 g/8 oz plain flour	2 cups all-purpose flour
500 g/1¼ lb wholemeal flour	4½ cups wholewheat flour
1 x 2.5 ml spoon/½ teaspoon salt	½ teaspoon salt
75 g/3 oz butter	6 tablespoons butter
50 g/2 oz tinned anchovies, drained and chopped	2 oz canned anchovies, drained and chopped

*If using dried or easy-blend yeast, use 15 g/½ oz/1 tablespoon.
Note: combine easy-blend yeast with the flours before adding the liquid.*

Makes a 1 kg/ 2 lb loaf

Preparation time: 15 minutes

Rising time: about 1½ hours

Cooking time: about 40 minutes

Oven: 220° C, 425°F, Gas Mark 7

1 Mix the water, milk, fresh yeast and sugar in a bowl. Leave to froth up.
2 Sift the flours and salt into a separate mixing bowl.
3 Melt the butter in a small pan and heat until nut-brown. Stir into the yeast liquid.
4 Make a well in the centre of the flour mixture and pour in sufficient of the combined liquids to form a soft, but not sticky, dough. Gradually incorporate the flour until a dough is formed. Turn out on to a floured board and knead until the dough is firm and springy. Place in a greased bowl and turn the ball of dough over.
5 Sprinkle the chopped anchovies on top of the dough, cover the basin with a cloth and leave to prove in a warm place for 1 hour.
6 Knead the dough again, then place in a greased 1 kg/2 lb loaf tin. Cover and leave in a warm place to prove until fully risen.
7 Place in a preheated oven and bake for approximately 20 minutes. Cover with foil and continue baking for a further 20 minutes. Turn out on to a rack to cool completely.

Olive and Onion Bread

METRIC/IMPERIAL	AMERICAN
40 g/1½ oz fresh yeast*	1½ oz fresh yeast*
1 x 2.5 ml spoon/½ teaspoon caster sugar	½ teaspoon granulated sugar
275 ml/9 fl oz warm water	1 cup plus 2 tablespoons warm water
450 g/1lb strong white flour	1 lb bread flour
1 x 7.5 ml spoon/1½ teaspoons salt	1½ teaspoons salt
24 green olives, stoned and finely chopped	24 green olives, stoned and finely chopped
½ onion, finely chopped	½ onion, finely chopped

*If using dried yeast, use 1 teaspoon yeast. For easy-blend dried yeast, use 1 sachet and mix with the flour, not with the liquid.

Serves 4

Preparation time: 10 minutes

Resting time: about 2 hours

Cooking time: 20-25 minutes

1 Mix the fresh (or regular dried) yeast with the sugar and water in a bowl and stir well to dissolve.
2 Sift the flour and salt into a large bowl. Make a well in the centre and add the yeast mixture which should be frothy. Mix to a dough and knead on a floured board, by hand, for about 7 minutes. If the dough seems too wet, mix in a little more flour.
3 When the dough is elastic and 'live' feeling, place in a greased bowl and sprinkle with the chopped olives and onions. Turn over so that all sides of the dough ball glisten. Cover the bowl with a cloth or cling film (saran wrap), and leave to rise in a warm place for about 1 hour.
4 When the dough has doubled in size, knock it down, and mix with your hands to ensure that the olives and onions are well mixed in.

In The Shooting Lodge: Country Pâté.   Veal and Ham Pie   Olive and Onion Bread
Roast Chicken   Roast Sirloin of Beef

Oven: 230°C, 450°F,
Gas Mark 8

5 Turn the dough out on to a floured board and flatten it into a large disc, about 2.5 cm/1 inch thick. Transfer to a greased baking (cookie) sheet. Cover with oiled cling film (saran wrap) and leave to rise in a warm place for about 1 hour.
6 Bake in a preheated oven for 20-25 minutes. Transfer from the baking (cookie) sheet to a rack and leave to cool.

Roast Sirloin of Beef

METRIC/IMPERIAL

AMERICAN

50 g/2 oz margarine
1 x 1 kg/2 lb joint of beef sirloin,
boned, rolled and tied
salt and pepper
1 onion, roughly chopped
1 large carrot, roughly chopped

4 tablespoons margarine
2 lb sirloin roast, boned,
rolled and tied
salt and pepper
1 onion, roughly chopped
1 large carrot, roughly chopped

Serves 6-8

Preparation time:
5 minutes

Cooking time:
2 hours 20 minutes
Oven: 230°C, 450°F, Gas Mark 8

1 Melt the margarine in a flameproof roasting tin. Put in the beef, turn and baste on all sides. Remove from the tin and season.
2 Add the chopped vegetables to the roasting tin and place the joint on top (this will prevent the meat from overcooking).
3 Roast the joint in a preheated oven, allowing 15 minutes per pound and 15 minutes over. Remove from the oven and leave to cool completely.

Pigeon (Squab) Breast with Walnut and Orange Vinaigrette

METRIC/IMPERIAL	AMERICAN
25 g/1 oz butter	*2 tablespoons butter*
2 medium-sized oven-ready pigeons	*2 medium-sized oven-ready squabs, squab chickens or fresh Rock Cornish hens*
assorted salad (lamb's lettuce, lollo rosso, etc)	*assorted salad (arugula, radicchio, Bibb lettuce, chicory)*

Vinaigrette

1 dessertspoon white wine vinegar	*1½ teaspoons white wine vinegar*
1 egg yolk, size 1, beaten	*1 jumbo egg yolk, beaten*
1 x 5 ml spoon/1 teaspoon Dijon mustard	*1 teaspoon Dijon or other mild mustard*
1 dessertspoon frozen concentrated orange juice (thawed)	*1½ teaspoons frozen orange juice concentrate (thawed)*
300 ml/½ pint walnut oil	*1¼ cups walnut oil*
salt and pepper	*salt and pepper*

Note: the remaining Orange and Walnut vinaigrette can be kept in a tightly stoppered bottle in a cool place for at least 1 week. Shake well before using.

Serves 4

Preparation time: 15 minutes

Cooking time: 20-25 minutes

Oven: 230°C, 450°F, Gas Mark 8

1 Melt the butter in a roasting pan. Fry the pigeons (squab or Rock cornish hens) until golden brown on all sides.

2 Roast on a rack in a preheated oven for 12 – 15 minutes, then remove and leave to cool completely.

3 To make the vinaigrette, mix together the white wine vinegar, egg yolk, mustard and concentrated orange juice. Whisk until all the ingredients are thoroughly combined. Gradually add the walnut oil, whisking constantly, until completely incorporated. Season with salt and pepper. Wash the salad greens and put in a bowl.

4 With a small sharp pointed knife remove the legs of the birds, then remove the breasts. Make an incision down the side of the backbone and, with long sweeping cuts, remove the flesh from the bone, following the contours of the carcass.

5 Cut each breast into 5 equal pieces and arrange on a plate in a fan shape. Measure out 150 ml/5 fl oz /a generous ½ cup of the dressing into a small jug (pitcher). Pour a dessertspoon over the salad, mix well, season and place a small mound of salad on each plate. Spoon a little of the remaining vinaigrette over the pigeon (squab or Rock Cornish hen) breasts.

Langoustine Brochettes with a Cream Oyster Sauce

METRIC/IMPERIAL	AMERICAN
24 x 25 g/1 oz pieces of langoustine tails, shelled	24 x 1 oz pieces of rock lobster tails, shelled
½ egg white, size 4, lightly beaten	1 very small egg white, lightly beaten
50 ml/2 fl oz double cream	¼ cup heavy cream
salt and pepper	salt and pepper
40 g/1½ oz sesame seeds	2 level tablespoons sesame seeds
40 g/1½ oz butter	2½ tablespoons butter
4 sprigs chervil, to garnish	4 sprigs chervil, to garnish

Sauce

METRIC/IMPERIAL	AMERICAN
25 g/1 oz butter	2 tablespoons butter
1 shallot, finely minced	1 shallot, finely minced
50 ml/2 fl oz dry white wine	¼ cup dry white wine
2 oysters	2 oysters
175 ml/6 fl oz double cream	¾ cup heavy cream
salt and pepper	salt and pepper
⅛ teaspoon (pinch) grated fresh ginger	⅛ teaspoon (pinch) grated fresh ginger

Serves 4

Preparation time: about 30 minutes

Cooking time: 15 minutes

Oven: 200°C, 400°F, Gas Mark 6

1 For each serving, lay 6 pieces of langoustine (rock lobster) tail side by side and run a wooden skewer through them. Trim off the edges so that they are even. Chill all the langoustine trimmings.

2 Purée the trimmings in a food processor as smooth as possible.

3 Put the langoustine purée in a bowl and set over a container of crushed ice. Beat in the egg white, a little at a time, until completely mixed. Add the double (heavy) cream gradually in about 6 stages. Beat well between each stage. When the mixture is mousse-like, season to taste.

4 Smooth the mousse over the skewered langoustine (rock lobster) tails, with a palette knife (spatula), to make a smooth even surface on all sides, filling any gaps.

5 Roll the mousse-covered tails in the sesame seeds, coating evenly. (Have another 25 g/1 oz/1 tablespoon of seeds ready to use if necessary.)

6 Melt the butter in a heavy ovenproof pan and cook the tails until golden brown on one side. Turn and brown the other side. Place the pan in a preheated oven and cook for 4- 5 minutes.

7 To make the sauce, melt the butter in a pan. Add the shallots and cook, without colouring, for 1-2 minutes.

8 Add the white wine and cook briskly until the liquid is reduced by half.

9 Chop the oysters finely, then press through a sieve to make a purée. Stir into the sauce, blend, then add the double (heavy) cream.

10 Bring the sauce to the boil and reduce by a further third. Add salt and pepper and the grated ginger. Remove from the heat and leave the ginger to infuse for 2-3 minutes. The sauce should coat the back of a spoon.

11 Strain the sauce into a clean bowl. Pour about 50 ml/2 fl oz/4 tablespoons of sauce on to each plate, covering the whole surface.

12 Lay a skewer of langoustine (rock lobster) tails on the sauce, gently pulling out the skewer. Garnish with sprigs of chervil.

Apricot and Apple Pastry

METRIC/IMPERIAL AMERICAN

METRIC/IMPERIAL	AMERICAN
20 g/¾ oz butter	1 tablespoon plus 1 teaspoon butter
4 crisp eating apples, peeled, cored and sliced	4 crisp eating apples, peeled, cored and sliced
75 g/3 oz caster sugar	scant ½ cup superfine or granulated sugar
juice of 1 lemon	juice of 1 lemon
1 x 1.25 ml spoon/good pinch of ground cinnamon	good pinch of powdered cinnamon
4 ripe apricots, peeled, halved and sliced	4 ripe apricots, peeled, halved and sliced
175 g/6 oz Puff pastry (opposite)	⅜ lb Puff pastry (opposite)
2 tablespoons milk	2 tablespoons milk
icing sugar, for dusting	confectioners' (powdered) sugar, for dusting
250 ml/8 fl oz Sauce anglaise (below)	1 cup Sauce anglaise (below)

To decorate

raspberries	raspberries
mint leaves	mint leaves

Serves 4

Preparation time: 20 minutes

Cooking time: 35 minutes

Oven: 230°C, 450°F, Gas Mark 8

1 Melt the butter in a saucepan and add the apple slices, sugar, lemon juice and cinnamon. Cover and cook gently for 10 – 15 minutes until tender, but not soft. Transfer to a large sieve or colander and leave to drain and cool.

2 Mix the apricots with the apples.

3 Roll out the pastry to a rectangle 20 x 23 cm/8 x 9 inches. Transfer the pastry to the reverse side of a large baking (cookie) sheet. Spread the apple and apricot mixture on the pastry, almost up to the edges, and roll up from one shorter side, Swiss roll (jelly roll) style. The diameter of the roll will be about 6 cm/2½ inches.

4 Brush the roll with milk and bake on the baking (cookie) sheet for approximately 20 minutes. Remove from the oven and leave to cool.

5 Dust the baked roll with sieved icing (confectioners') sugar and make a decorative pattern on the pastry with a hot skewer. Trim the ends of the roll obliquely, then cut the pastry into 4 portions, also at an oblique angle.

6 Place each portion on a plate and pour a little Sauce anglaise on the side. Decorate with raspberries and mint leaves.

Sauce Anglaise

METRIC/IMPERIAL	AMERICAN
150 ml/5 fl oz milk	½ cup plus 4 tablespoons milk
75 ml/2½ fl oz double cream	5 tablespoons heavy cream
zest of ½ small lemon	zest of ½ small lemon
zest of ½ small orange	zest of ½ small orange
3 egg yolks, size 2	3 large egg yolks
50 g/2 oz caster sugar	4 tablespoons superfine or granulated sugar

Makes 400 ml/ scant 15 fl oz/ scant pint (US)

Preparation time: 5 minutes

Cooking time: 15 minutes

1 Mix the milk, cream, lemon and orange zest and half the sugar in a heavy-based pan and bring gently to simmering point.

2 Whisk the egg yolks and remaining sugar together until light and fluffy. Pour the hot milk mixture gradually on to the egg and sugar, beating constantly.

3 Place the pan over a high heat and bring just to simmering point, stirring constantly and reaching all around the pan with the spoon. The sauce must not boil. Heat until the mixture coats the back of a metal spoon. If it is too thin, lower the heat and simmer gently to a coating consistency.

4 Strain into a bowl and leave to cool. The sauce will keep for 3 days in the refrigerator, with a sheet of cling film pressed on to the surface and the bowl tightly covered with extra cling film (saran wrap).

Apricot and Apple Pastry

Puff Pastry

METRIC/IMPERIAL

AMERICAN

225 g/8 oz plain flour
salt
225 g/8 oz margarine or
butter, very cold
150 ml/¼ pint ice-cold water

few drops of lemon juice

½ lb (1½ cups) all-purpose flour
salt
½ lb margarine or butter,
very cold
generous ½ cup (5 fl oz) ice-cold
water
few drops of lemon juice

Note: care must be taken when rolling out the paste to keep the ends and sides square. The lightness of the paste is caused by the air which is trapped when folding the pastry during preparation.

**Makes 500 g/
1¼ lb**

**Preparation time:
20 minutes**

**Resting time:
1 hour 50 minutes**

1 Sift the flour and salt into a bowl. Rub or cut in with a pastry blender, 50 g/2 oz/ 4 tablespoons of the fat.
2 Make a well in the centre and add the water and lemon juice. Knead well into a smooth dough to form a ball. Leave the dough to rest in a cool place for 30 minutes.
3 Cut a cross half way through the dough and pull out the corners to form a star shape. Roll out the points of the star square, leaving the centre thick.
4 Knead the remaining fat to the same texture as the dough. (This is most important: if the fat is too soft it will melt and ooze out, if too hard it will break through the paste when being rolled.)
5 Place the fat on the thick centre of the star shape and fold over the flaps. Roll out to approximately 30 x 15 cm/12 x 6 inches, cover with a cloth and leave to rest in a cool place for 20 minutes.
6 Roll out to approximately 60 x 20 cm/24 x 8 inches, fold both ends into the centre and fold in half again to form a square – this is one double turn. Leave to rest in a cool place for 20 minutes.
7 Half turn the paste to the right or left and roll out again. Give one more double turn (Step 6), roll out and leave to rest for 20 minutes. Give the pastry 2 more double turns, rolling out and resting between each turn. Leave to rest for another 20 minutes before using.

91

Smoked Crab and Chicory (Endive) Salad with Chive Mayonnaise

	METRIC/IMPERIAL	AMERICAN
	8 medium-sized chicory spears	8 medium-size endive spears
	250 ml/8 fl oz fresh orange juice	1 cup fresh orange juice
	salt and pepper	salt and pepper
Chive mayonnaise	½ bunch chives, chopped	½ bunch chives, chopped
	225 g/8 oz mayonnaise	1 cup mayonnaise
	2 tomatoes, peeled and finely diced	2 tomatoes, peeled and diced
	120 ml/4 fl oz double cream	½ cup heavy cream
	225 g/8 oz smoked crabmeat	1 cup smoked crabmeat
To garnish	4 sprigs chervil	4 sprigs chervil
	1 large carrot, shredded	1 large carrot, shredded

Serves 4

Preparation time: 20 minutes

Cooling time: 1 hour

1 With a stainless steel knife, and working from the point to the base, shred the chicory (endive) spears as finely as possible. Place in a bowl.

2 Pour the orange juice into a pan and bring to the boil. Boil until reduced by half. Leave until cold. Pour this concentrated orange juice over the chicory (endive).

3 Season with salt and pepper and chill in a refrigerator for 1 hour.

4 To make the chive mayonnaise: mix the chives, mayonnaise, tomato and double (heavy) cream and season with salt and pepper.

5 Place a 10 cm/4 inch round pastry cutter in the centre of a dinner plate. Spoon a little of the endive salad into the ring and level off.

6 Spoon 2-3 teaspoons of smoked crabmeat on top and spread evenly.

7 Pour about 50 ml/2 fl oz/4 tablespoons of chive mayonnaise around the ring, covering the rest of the plate.

8 Remove the pastry cutter carefully and garnish each serving with a sprig of chervil and a little shredded carrot.

Studded Collops of Beef with Marinated Grapes

	METRIC/IMPERIAL	AMERICAN
	40 g/1½ oz Clarified butter (page 94)	3 tablespoons Clarified butter (page 94)
	1.25 kg/2½ lb sirloin of beef, boned, rolled and larded with pork fat by your butcher	2½ lb sirloin roast of beef, boned, rolled and larded with pork fat by your butcher
	salt and pepper	salt and pepper
Red wine sauce	15g/½ oz butter	1 tablespoon butter
	25 g/1 oz shallots, chopped	1 rounded tablespoon shallots, chopped
	½ teaspoon thyme and tarragon, mixed and chopped	½ teaspoon thyme and tarragon, mixed and chopped
	85 ml/3 fl oz red wine	6 tablespoons red wine
	450 ml/¾ pint Beef stock (page 94)	scant pint (15 fl oz) Beef stock (page 94)
	salt and pepper	salt and pepper

Marinated grapes	85 ml/3 fl oz red wine	*6 tablespoons red wine*
	4 small bunches black grapes	*4 small bunches black grapes*
To garnish	1 small carrot, peeled and	*1 small carrot, peeled and*
	cut into 4 or 5 rings, core	*cut into 4 or 5 rings, core*
	removed, blanched	*removed, blanched*
	4-5 sprigs watercress	*4-5 sprigs watercress*

**Serves 4
(generously)**

**Preparation time:
20 minutes**

**Cooking time:
50 minutes**

**Resting time:
5-10 minutes**

**Oven: 240°C, 475°F,
Gas Mark 9**

1 Heat the clarified butter in a roasting tin and seal the beef on all sides.

2 Rub the beef with salt and pepper and roast in a preheated oven for 40 minutes, turning every 10 minutes so that it cooks evenly. When cooked, remove from the oven and leave to rest for 5-10 minutes before carving.

3 To make the sauce, melt the 15 g/1½ oz/1 tablespoon butter in a saucepan. Add the shallots and herbs and sauté for 2 minutes.

4 Add the wine and reduce by two-thirds.

5 Add the stock and reduce by half again. Strain and season to taste. Keep warm.

6 Warm the bunches of grapes in the 85 ml/3 fl oz/6 tablespoons red wine, over gentle heat.

7 For each portion, carve 2 slices of beef approximately 2 cm/¾ inch thick. Arrange on a warmed dinner plate and place a bunch of the marinated grapes next to the beef. Pour on a little red wine sauce.

8 To garnish each serving, place a sprig of watercress through a carrot ring.

Smoked Crab and Chicory (Endive) Salad with Chive Mayonnaise   Studded Collops of Beef with Marinated Grapes

Beef Stock

METRIC/IMPERIAL

METRIC/IMPERIAL	AMERICAN
1 kg/2 lb raw beef bones	2 lb raw beef bones
225 g/8 oz vegetables	½ lb vegetables
(carrots, onions, celery, leeks)	(carrots, onions, celery, leeks)
bouquet garni (thyme, bay leaf,	bouquet garni (thyme, bay leaf,
parsley stalks)	parsley stalks)
6 black peppercorns	6 black peppercorns
2 level dessertspoons salt	4 teaspoons salt

**Makes 1.75 litres/
3 pints/
4 pints (US)**

**Cooking time:
8-9 hours**

**Oven: 220°C, 425° F,
Gas Mark 7**

1 Chop the bones and brown well on all sides by one of 2 methods: a) place in a roasting tin in a preheated oven for 45 minutes, or b) brown carefully for 10 minutes in a little fat in a frying pan.
2 Drain off any fat and put the bones in a stock pot. Set the roasting tin or frying pan over high heat, and brown the remaining sediment, scraping it from the bottom of the pan with a wooden spoon. Pour in 300 ml/½ pint/1¼ cups of water and simmer for a few minutes, then add to the bones. Do not discard the water. Add 2.25 litres/4 pints/5 pints (US) water. Bring to the boil and skim well.
3 Wash, peel and roughly chop the vegetables and gently fry in a little hot oil or fat until brown. Strain off the fat and add the vegetables to the stock pot. Add the bouquet garni, peppercorns and salt and simmer for 6-8 hours (2 hours for chicken stock). Skim off any froth that rises to the top from time to time. At the end of the cooking time, skim again thoroughly, strain and cool. This stock will keep 3-4 days in a refrigerator, or 2 months if frozen.

Clarified Butter

**Makes 500 g/1¼ lb/
20 oz**

1 Melt 1 kg/2 lb/32 oz salted butter in a small pan and cook over a gentle heat, without stirring, until the butter begins to foam. Continue to cook the butter without browning until the foaming stops.
2 Remove the pan from the heat and let it stand until the milky deposits have sunk to the bottom, leaving a clear yellow liquid.
3 Pour this liquid carefully through a double layer of muslin wrung out in warm water into a bowl.
Clarified butter can be stored in a refrigerator for up to 6 weeks and can be used in liquid or solid form.

Fig Mousse and Mango Sorbet

METRIC/IMPERIAL	AMERICAN
3-4 large fresh figs,	3-4 large fresh figs,
thinly sliced	thinly sliced
2 egg yolks size 1, or	2 jumbo egg yolks, or
3 yolks, size 3	3 large yolks
40 g/1½ oz caster sugar	3 level tablespoons superfine sugar
2 x 5 ml spoons/2 level	2 level teaspoons powdered
teaspoons powdered gelatine	gelatin
100 ml/4 fl oz milk	½ cup milk
175 ml/6 fl oz double cream,	1 cup heavy cream,
softly whipped	softly whipped
Ginger coulis (opposite)	Ginger coulis (opposite)

**Mango
sorbet**

250 ml/8 fl oz mango purée	1 cup mango purée
(see method)	(see method)
250 ml/8 fl oz Stock syrup	1 cup Stock syrup
(opposite)	(opposite)
1 egg white, size 3,	1 large egg white,
lightly beaten	lightly beaten

To decorate	175 g/6 oz fresh strawberries or raspberries	*1½ cups fresh strawberries or raspberries*
	1 x 15 ml spoon/1 tablespoon chopped sugared ginger	*1 tablespoon candied ginger, chopped*

Kiwi fruit can be substituted if fresh figs are difficult to obtain.

Serves 4

1 You will need 4 deep saucers. Line the inside surfaces of the saucers with the fig (or kiwi) slices.

Preparation time: 1 hour

2 Whisk the egg yolks and sugar together until light and fluffy.

3 Dissolve the gelatine in about 15 ml/1 tablespoon water, set in a saucepan of hot water and stir until completely clear.

Chilling time: 4 hours

4 Heat the milk until steaming, then pour on to the whisked egg yolks and sugar, whisking constantly. Return the mixture to the pan and heat gently, stirring constantly, until the mixture barely touches simmering point. Do not allow the mixture to boil or it will curdle.

Freezing time: 30 minutes

5 When the custard is hot and thickened, remove it promptly from the heat and stir in the dissolved gelatine. Sit the base of the pan in cold water and leave, stirring occasionally, until cooled and thickened, but not set.

6 Fold in the softly whipped cream, pour into the fig-lined dishes and leave to set in the refrigerator for about 4 hours.

7 Meanwhile, prepare the mango purée: use tinned mango slices, drained and liquidized or whirled in a food processor, or very ripe fresh mangoes, peeled, sliced and puréed.

8 Mix the mango purée and stock syrup together and pour into an ice-cream or sorbet maker and freeze to a slush (following the manufacturer's instructions). When the sorbet is slushy, turn into a bowl and add the lightly beaten egg white. Freeze for about 30 minutes.

9 While the sorbet is freezing, make the ginger coulis (see opposite) and leave to cool until syrupy, but not set.

10 To serve, carefully invert each mousse in the centre of a dessert plate. Pour a border of ginger coulis around the mousse. Spoon or pipe a portion of mango sorbet on top of the mousse. Decorate with berries and sugared (candied) ginger.

Stock Syrup

METRIC/IMPERIAL	AMERICAN
225 g/8 oz caster sugar	*1 cup superfine or granulated sugar*
300 ml/½ pint water	*1¼ cups water*
juice of 1 lemon	*juice of 1 lemon*
juice of 1 orange	*juice of 1 orange*

Makes 450 ml/ ¾ pint/ scant pint (15 fl oz) (US)

1 Combine all the ingredients in a saucepan and boil until all the sugar has completely dissolved.

2 Strain and leave to cool. Store in a tightly stoppered bottle in the refrigerator.

Preparation time: 20 minutes

Ginger Coulis

METRIC/IMPERIAL	AMERICAN
200 ml/⅓ pint Stock syrup (above)	*⅞ cup (7 fl oz) Stock syrup (above)*
15 g/1 tablespoon ground ginger	*1 tablespoon powdered ginger*
15 g/1 tablespoon powdered gelatine	*1 tablespoon gelatin powder*

Makes 200 ml/ ⅓ pint/7 fl oz

1 Mix the stock syrup and ground ginger in a small pan and bring to the boil.

2 Dissolve the gelatine in the hot mixture. Remove from the heat, strain and leave to cool.

WINTER

Winter at Gleneagles evokes images of snow-capped hills,
frost-edged greens and cosy interiors.
Even when the weather does not permit outdoor activities,
Gleneagles has much to offer as an indoor resort.
Table tennis, billiards, squash or a work-out
in the gymnasium can all be enjoyed without setting foot
outside the Hotel, and, of course, a swim in
the heated pool, followed by a sauna and massage,
is an ideal tonic for Winter blues.

Winter dishes are usually richer than at other times
of the year, and dining a more leisurely affair,
enjoyed on a rainy day or over a long Winter evening.
The Chef's Winter selection includes
an impressive roast beef course and a special
spaghetti dish as well as a traditional fireside tea
and dramatic flambé desserts.

The menus are perfect for entertaining, whether
organising an elegant cocktail party, or serving your
guests a hearty Scottish breakfast the morning after!

By the fireside in The Shooting Lodge

Crusted Pheasant Terrine

Vegetables with Soya (Soy) Sauce and Saffron Rice

Chocolate Truffle Gâteau with Fresh Cream

Crusted Pheasant Terrine

	METRIC/IMPERIAL	AMERICAN
Pastry	65 ml/2½ fl oz water	5 tablespoons water
	25 g/1 oz lard	2 tablespoons lard
	pinch of salt	pinch of salt
	100 g/4 oz plain flour	1 cup all-purpose flour
Filling	3 boneless pheasant breasts	3 boneless pheasant breasts
	½ sprig thyme, chopped	½ sprig thyme, chopped
	½ leaf tarragon, chopped	½ leaf tarragon, chopped
	1½ sprigs chervil, chopped	1½ sprigs chervil, chopped
	½ bay leaf, crumbled	½ bay leaf, crumbled
	salt and pepper	salt and pepper
	85 ml/3 fl oz dry white wine	6 tablespoons dry white wine
	40 g/1½ oz pistachio nuts, peeled and blanched	generous ¼ cup pistachio nuts, peeled and blanched
Garlic croûtons	25 g/1 oz butter	2 tablespoons butter
	1 garlic clove, peeled and finely chopped	1 garlic clove, peeled and finely chopped
	1 slice white bread, crusts removed and cut into 5 mm/¼ inch dice	1 slice white bread, crusts removed and cut into ¼ inch dice
Port jelly	85 ml/3 fl oz water	scant ½ cup water
	2 x 5 ml spoons/2 teaspoons powdered gelatine	2 teaspoons gelatin powder
	50 ml/2 fl oz port	¼ cup port
To serve	assorted salad greens	assorted salad greens
	chopped hazelnuts	chopped hazelnuts

Serves 4-6

Preparation time: 30 minutes

Marinating time: 24 hours

Cooking time: about 1 hour

Oven: 180°C, 350°F, Gas Mark 4

1 To make the pastry, place the water, lard and salt in a pan and bring to the boil. Add the flour and mix to a smooth dough. Remove from the heat and turn into a bowl to cool completely.

2 Sprinkle the pheasant supremes with the thyme, tarragon, chervil and bay leaf. Season with salt and pepper. Moisten with the white wine and place in a refrigerator container. Cover tightly and leave to marinate for 24 hours in the refrigerator.

3 On a lightly floured board, roll out the pastry thinly and cut into 2 rectangles, one large enough to line the sides of a 450 g/1 lb terrine and the other of a size to make a lid for the pâté.

4 Line the terrine with the larger pastry rectangle, bringing the pastry up slightly higher than the edge. Lay 1 pheasant supreme on the bottom and sprinkle with one-third of the pistachios. Add another 2 layers of pheasant and pistachios.

5 Lay the pastry lid on the terrine and crimp the edges together firmly, moistening with cold water if necessary, to make them stick together. Pierce 2 holes 1 cm/½ inch in diameter in the top of the pastry. Place in a preheated oven and cook for 50 minutes – 1 hour, until a skewer inserted through a hole into the centre of the terrine comes out clean.

6 To make the garlic croûtons, melt the butter in a frying pan and add the garlic. Fry the bread cubes slowly, stirring, until golden brown. Drain on paper towels.

7 To prepare the port jelly, bring the water to the boil and add the gelatine. Remove from the heat. When the gelatine is dissolved, add the port.

8 When the terrine is cooked, remove from the oven and pour the port jelly through the holes in the pastry lid. Leave to cool completely.

9 Serve the terrine in slices with assorted green salads mixed with chopped hazelnuts, and the garlic croûtons sprinkled over the top.

Crusted Pheasant Terrine   Vegetables with Soya (Soy) Sauce and Saffron Rice

Vegetables with Soya (Soy) Sauce and Saffron Rice

METRIC/IMPERIAL	AMERICAN
25 g/1 oz butter	*2 tablespoons butter*
1 small cauliflower, divided into florets	*1 small cauliflower, divided into florets*
1 small head broccoli, divided into florets	*1 small head broccoli, divided into florets*
10 baby carrots, peeled and halved lengthways	*10 baby carrots, peeled and halved lengthwise*
1 large courgette, roughly chopped	*1 large zucchini, roughly chopped*
½ small green pepper, cored, seeded and chopped	*½ small green pepper, cored, seeded and chopped*
½ small red pepper, cored, seeded and chopped	*½ small red pepper, cored, seeded and chopped*
4 ears baby corn, halved lengthways	*4 ears baby corn, halved lengthwise*
50 ml/2 fl oz soya sauce	*¼ cup soy sauce*
120 ml/4 fl oz Beef glaze (page 102)	*½ cup Beef glaze (page 102)*

	METRIC/IMPERIAL	AMERICAN
Saffron rice	50 g/2 oz butter	*4 tablespoons butter*
	1 medium onion, peeled and chopped	*1 medium onion, peeled and chopped*
	250 g/9 oz long-grain rice	*1½ cups long-grain rice*
	good pinch of saffron strands	*good pinch of saffron strands*
	400 ml/14 fl oz chicken or	*1¾ cups chicken or*
	vegetable stock	*vegetable stock*
	salt and pepper	*salt and pepper*

Serves 4

Preparation time: 5 minutes

Cooking time: 45 minutes

Oven: 200°C°, 400°F, Gas Mark 6

1 Melt the butter in a heavy-based saucepan or casserole. Add the vegetables and cover. Cook over a low heat for 10 minutes, stirring occasionally to prevent the vegetables from sticking.
2 Add the soya (soy) sauce and beef glaze and simmer for a further 5 minutes until the vegetables are tender, but not soft.
3 To prepare the rice, melt 40 g/1½ oz/2½ tablespoons butter in an ovenproof dish or casserole, add the onion and cook gently, without colouring, for 2–3 minutes. Add the rice, saffron, stock, salt and pepper, stir well and bring to the boil.
4 Cover the dish and place in a preheated oven for 15–20 minutes. Remove from the oven, stir in the remaining butter and adjust the seasoning.
5 Serve the vegetables and rice in separate dishes.

Chocolate Truffle Gâteau with Fresh Cream

	METRIC/IMPERIAL	AMERICAN
Sponge cake (Genoese)	2 eggs, size 1	*2 jumbo eggs*
	50 g/2 oz caster sugar	*4 tablespoons superfine or granulated sugar*
	40 g/1½ oz (4 tablespoons) flour	*4 tablespoons all-purpose flour*
	15 g/½ oz (1 teaspoon) cocoa powder	*1 teaspoon cocoa powder*
	25 g/1 oz butter, melted	*2 tablespoons butter, melted*
Filling	90 g/3 oz white chocolate (Milky Bar), broken into pieces	*3 oz white dessert chocolate, broken into pieces*
	150 g/5 oz plain dark chocolate (Bournville), broken into pieces	*5 oz (5 squares) semi-sweet chocolate (Bakers'), broken into pieces*
	15 g/½ oz unsalted butter	*1 tablespoon unsalted butter*
	2 egg yolks, size 3, beaten	*2 medium egg yolks, beaten*
	25 ml/1 fl oz whisky	*2 tablespoons Scotch whisky*
	25 ml/1 fl oz double cream	*2 tablespoons heavy cream*
	2 egg whites, size 3, stiffly beaten	*2 medium egg whites, stiffly beaten*

Serves 8

Preparation time: 20-25 minutes

Cooking time: 30 – 35 minutes

Setting time: overnight

Oven: 180°C, 350°F, Gas Mark 4

1 To make the sponge cake (Genoese), whisk the eggs and sugar over a pan of hot water until light and fluffy. Sift the flour and cocoa powder together.
2 Very gently fold the flour/cocoa mixture into the egg and sugar, then trickle the melted butter around the edges and gently stir until just mixed.
3 Grease a 15 cm/6 inch round, 7.5 cm/3 inch deep sandwich (layer cake) tin and line with silicone or waxed paper. Pour in the mixture. Place in a preheated oven and bake for 30 minutes. Remove from the oven, leave to cool slightly in the tin, then turn out on to a rack.
4 Melt the chocolate with the butter in the top of a double boiler. Do not let steam or water enter the chocolate.
5 Whisk the egg yolks and whisky into the chocolate mixture, then mix in the cream. Tip a tablespoon or two of the chocolate mixture into the bowl of beaten egg whites, gently fold together, then fold in the remaining chocolate mixture until it is of a mousse-like consistency.
6 Line a 15 cm/6 inch loose-bottomed cake tin with silicone or waxed paper. Cut the top off the chocolate cake (about 5mm/¼ inch thick) and lay cut-side down in the base of the tin. Cut the cake across into 5 mm/¼ inch thick strips and use to line the sides of the tin, 2 strips deep. Pour in the chocolate mousse, leave in the refrigerator for a few minutes, then cover the top with the remaining cake strips. Cover with cling film (saran wrap) and leave to set overnight in the refrigerator.
7 Carefully remove the gâteau from the cake tin (invert on to a serving plate) and cut into 1 cm/½ inch slices – it is very rich. Serve with double (heavy) cream. Any leftover gâteau can be kept in the refrigerator for up to 4 days, or frozen.

Cream of Chicken Soup with Sorrel and Fine Pasta

Roast Sirloin of Beef with Asparagus Mousse and Red Wine Sauce

Black Cherries flamed in Kirsch   or

Sugared Bananas flamed in White Rum

Cream of Chicken Soup with Sorrel and Fine Pasta

METRIC/IMPERIAL	AMERICAN
20 g/¾ oz butter	*1½ tablespoons butter*
40 g/1½ oz celery,	*1 small stick celery,*
trimmed and roughly chopped	*trimmed and roughly chopped*
40 g/1½ oz leeks, well	*1 small leek, well washed and*
washed and roughly chopped	*roughly chopped*
(white part only)	*(white part only)*
40 g/1½ oz onion, peeled and	*1 small onion, peeled and*
roughly chopped	*roughly chopped*
175 g/6 oz raw chicken bones, chopped	*6 oz raw chicken bones, chopped*
25 g/1 oz plain flour	*3 level tablespoons all-purpose flour*
600 ml/1 pint cold	*1¼ pints cold Chicken*
Chicken stock (page 117)	*stock (page 117)*
6 sorrel leaves, roughly chopped	*6 sorrel leaves, roughly chopped*
juice of 1 lemon	*juice of 1 lemon*
salt and pepper	*salt and pepper*
20 g/¾ oz fresh pasta vermicelli	*a small handful of fresh*
	vermicelli (fine noodles)
40 ml/1½ fl oz double cream	*3 tablespoons heavy cream*

Serves 4

**Preparation time:
15-20 minutes**

**Cooking time:
2½ hours**

**Oven: 180°C, 350°C,
Gas Mark 4**

1 Melt the butter in a heavy-based ovenproof saucepan or casserole and cook the celery, leek and onion for 1-2 minutes, without colouring.

2 Add the chicken bones and cook, stirring, without colouring, for 15 minutes. Stir in the flour.

3 Add the chicken stock very gradually, stirring constantly, until the mixture is smooth.

4 Add half the sorrel leaves to the soup and bring to the boil. Cover the pan and place in a preheated oven to cook slowly for about 2 hours. Remove and set aside to cool slightly.

5 Strain the soup into a clean pan and stir in the lemon juice. Mix well, correct the seasoning, and set on low heat to keep warm.

6 In another saucepan, bring 150 ml/¼ pint/a generous ½ cup of salted water to the boil. Add the vermicelli and cook for 5 minutes. Drain and set aside.

7 Shred the remaining sorrel leaves and divide them between 4 soup bowls. Add a heaped teaspoon of cooked vermicelli to each bowl.

8 Stir the double (heavy) cream into the soup and ladle into the bowls.

Roast Sirloin of Beef with Asparagus Mousse and Red Wine Sauce

METRIC/IMPERIAL	AMERICAN
1.5 kg/3 lb sirloin of beef,	*3 lb sirloin of beef, boned*
boned, trimmed, rolled and tied	*trimmed, rolled and tied*
salt and pepper	*salt and pepper*
40 ml/3 tablespoons vegetable oil	*3 tablespoons vegetable oil*

**Asparagus
mousse**

METRIC/IMPERIAL	AMERICAN
100 g/4 oz uncooked white	*4 oz uncooked white chicken*
chicken meat, trimmed	*meat, trimmed*
175 ml/6 fl oz double cream	*¾ cup heavy cream*
6 asparagus tips, cooked and puréed	*6 asparagus tips, cooked and puréed*

Sauce	350 ml/12 fl oz Beef glaze (below)	*1½ cups Beef glaze (below)*
	1 small onion, roughly chopped	*1 small onion, roughly chopped*
	3 mushrooms, roughly chopped	*3 mushrooms, roughly chopped*
	1 parsley stalk	*1 parsley stalk*
	65 ml//3 tablespoons dry red wine	*3 tablespoons dry red wine*

Serves 4

Preparation time:
30-35 minutes

Chilling time:
1 hour

Cooking time:
15 minutes per
450 g/1 lb (rare);
27 minutes per
450 g/1 lb (medium
rare)

Oven: 220°C, 425°F,
Gas Mark 7;
then: 160°C, 325°F,
Gas Mark 3

1 To make the asparagus mousse, finely process or mince (grind) the chicken and press through a fine sieve into a bowl. Place the bowl over another containing ice. Chill thoroughly for about 1 hour in the refrigerator.
2 Beat in the cream, in three or four even stages, to make a light mousse. Fold in the asparagus purée and salt and pepper to taste and mix well.
3 Preheat the oven to 220°C, 425°F, Gas Mark 7. Rub the beef with salt and pepper.
4 Heat the oil in a large flameproof roasting pan, until it begins to smoke. Seal the ends of the beef by standing the joint on each end in the hot oil. Seal each side.
5 Reduce the oven temperature to 160°C, 325°F, Gas Mark 3. Place the meat on a rack in the roasting tin and roast for 15 minutes per 450 g/1 lb for rare, or 27 minutes for medium rare beef. Turn the joint over halfway through the cooking time. Allow it to rest for 10 minutes, then cut into 8 slices, each approximately 5 mm/¼ inch thick.
6 Meanwhile, grease 4 dariole moulds, and spoon in the mousse, not quite to the top. Cover with cling film (saran wrap) and cook in a steamer for 10-12 minutes. The mousses are cooked when a knife inserted into the centre comes out clean.
7 For the sauce: put all the ingredients in a heavy-based pan, set over a low heat and reduce by one-third. Strain the sauce and season to taste.
8 For each portion, turn a mousse out on to a plate, place 2 slices of beef alongside and pour a border of sauce around the beef.

Beef Glaze

METRIC/IMPERIAL	AMERICAN
1.2 litres/2 pints Beef stock (page 94)	*2½ pints Beef stock (page 94)*
1 small onion, chopped	*1 small onion, chopped*
2 large mushrooms, washed and	*2 large mushrooms, washed and*
roughly chopped	*roughly chopped*
few parsley stalks	*few parsley stalks*
85 ml/3 fl oz dry red wine	*⅓ cup dry red wine*

Makes about 475 ml/
16-17 fl oz/1 pint (US)

1 Pour the beef stock into a large, heavy-based pan, set over a medium heat and reduce to one-quarter of its original volume: 300ml/½ pint/1¼ cups.
2 Add the chopped onions, mushrooms, parsley and wine and bring to the boil. Reduce the heat to a strong simmer and again reduce the volume by one-third.

Black Cherries flamed in Kirsch

METRIC/IMPERIAL	AMERICAN
50 g/2 oz butter	*4 tablespoons butter*
50 g/2 oz caster sugar	*4 tablespoons superfine or*
	granulated sugar
1 x 225 g/8 oz can black cherries	*1 x 8 oz can black cherries*
50 ml/2 fl oz Kirsch	*4 tablespoons Kirsch*
2 dessertspoons lime juice	*1½ tablespoons lime juice*
pinch of ground nutmeg	*pinch of ground nutmeg*

Serves 4

Preparation time:
5 minutes

Cooking time:
about 5 minutes

1 Melt the butter and sugar together in a flambé pan or small deep frying pan.
2 Stone the cherries. Reserve the syrup from the can.
3 Add the cherries and Kirsch to the butter and sugar mixture, light a match, stand back and ignite.
4 When the flame goes out, add the lime juice, nutmeg and syrup. Heat through.
5 Divide the cherries between individual plates or dishes, spoon a little syrup over each portion and serve with clotted cream, whipped cream or ice-cream. Alternatively, serve the cherries in Brandy snap baskets (page 124).

Sugared Bananas flamed in White Rum

METRIC/IMPERIAL	AMERICAN
75 g/3 oz butter	6 tablespoons butter
50 g/2 oz caster sugar	4 tablespoons superfine or granulated sugar
4 bananas, peeled and quartered lengthways	4 bananas, peeled and quartered lengthwise
50 ml/2 fl oz white rum	4 tablespoons white rum
juice of 2 oranges	juice of 2 oranges
juice of 1 lemon	juice of 1 lemon
ground cinnamon, for dusting	ground cinnamon, for dusting
4 strawberries, sliced	4 strawberries, sliced

Serves 4

Preparation time: 10 minutes

Cooking time: about 2 minutes

1 Melt the butter and sugar in a flambé pan or deep frying pan just large enough to contain the quartered bananas. Mix well and bring to the boil.

2 Add the bananas and turn them over in the mixture. Add the rum, light a match, stand back and ignite the rum.

3 When the flame goes out, add the orange and lemon juice. Dust the bananas with a little cinnamon and spoon the syrup over them to coat thoroughly.

4 Add the sliced strawberries and divide the fruit evenly between 4 dishes. Spoon a little syrup over each portion and serve at once, with whipped cream, clotted cream or ice-cream.

Black Cherries flamed in Kirsch

Sugared Bananas flamed in White Rum

Melon and Parma Ham (Prosciutto) Canapés

Baby Scallops   Smoked Salmon Canapés

Quails' Eggs and Caviar Canapés

Cured Beef and Baby Corn Canapés

Melon and Parma Ham (Prosciutto) Canapés

METRIC/IMPERIAL	AMERICAN
4 slices firm white bread, toasted	*4 slices firm white bread, toasted*
25 g/1 oz butter	*2 tablespoons butter*
12 thin slices Parma ham (prosciutto)	*12 thin slices prosciutto*
12 melon balls (Charentais, galia)	*12 melon balls (Cranshaw, honeydew, cantaloupe)*
75 g/3 oz mango chutney	*2 tablespoons mango chutney*
12 small sprigs parsley	*12 small sprigs parsley*

Makes 12

Preparation time: 5-10 minutes

1 Using a 3 cm/1¼ inch round cutter, cut out circles from the slices of toast.
2 Lightly butter the circles on one side only.
3 Wrap a slice of Parma ham (prosciutto) around a melon ball to form a collar. Place on a circle of toast and top with a little chutney.
4 Repeat the process for all circles, then decorate each with a sprig of parsley.

Baby Scallops

METRIC/IMPERIAL	AMERICAN
10 g/¼ oz butter	*½ tablespoon butter*
1 small shallot, peeled and chopped	*1 small shallot, peeled and chopped*
salt and pepper	*salt and pepper*
8 baby scallops, shelled, shells reserved	*8 baby scallops, shelled, shells reserved*
20 ml/1½ tablespoons dry white wine	*1½ tablespoons dry white wine*
10 ml/2 teaspoons brandy	*2 teaspoons brandy*
40 ml/2½ tablespoons double cream	*2½ tablespoons heavy cream*
1 teaspoon chopped chives	*1 teaspoon chopped chives*

Serves 4

Preparation time: 5 minutes

Cooking time: 6-8 minutes

1 Melt the butter in a pan, add the shallots and cook, without colouring, for 30 seconds.
2 Season the scallops and add to the shallots. Sauté for 15 seconds, then remove the scallops, using a slotted spoon.
3 Add the wine to the pan, bring to the boil and reduce by half. Add the brandy, stand back and ignite.
4 When the flame has gone out, add the cream to the pan and reduce the sauce by half its volume.
5 Return the scallops to the pan and gently reheat. Adjust the seasoning and add the chopped chives.
6 Place 2 scallops in the deeper half of each scallop shell and cover with sauce. Serve immediately.

*Cocktail Canapés
in Braid's:
Melon and Parma Ham
(Prosciutto)
Smoked Salmon
Quail's Eggs and Caviar
Cured Beef and Baby Corn
Baby Scallops*

Smoked Salmon Canapés

METRIC/IMPERIAL	AMERICAN
4 slices brown bread, toasted	*4 slices wholewheat bread, toasted*
25 g/1 oz butter	*2 tablespoons butter*
175 g/6 oz smoked salmon,	*6 oz smoked salmon,*
thinly sliced	*thinly sliced*
12 small sprigs chervil	*12 small sprigs chervil,*
	dill or watercress

Makes 12

***Preparation time:
5-8 minutes***

1 Using a 3 cm/1¼ inch round cutter, cut out circles from the slices of toast.
2 Lightly butter the circles on one side only.
3 Roll or fold the smoked salmon slices to fit exactly on the toast circles, and garnish with herb sprigs.

105

Quails' Eggs and Caviar Canapés

	METRIC/IMPERIAL	AMERICAN
Tartlet cases	225 g/8 oz plain flour	1½ cups all-purpose flour
	good pinch of salt	good pinch of salt
	50 g/2 oz lard	4 tablespoons lard
	50 g/2 oz butter	4 tablespoons butter
	cold water, for mixing	cold water, for mixing
Filling	4 x 5 ml spoons/4 teaspoons soured cream	4 teaspoons sour cream
	12 quails' eggs, hard-boiled, shelled and halved	12 quails' eggs, hard-boiled, shelled and halved
	4 x 5 ml spoons/4 teaspoons Beluga caviar	4 teaspoons Beluga caviar (or golden American caviar)
	12 small sprigs fresh dill	12 small sprigs fresh dill

Makes 12

Preparation time: 15 minutes

Cooking time: about 6 minutes

Oven: 180°C, 350°F, Gas Mark 4

1 To make the pastry, sift the flour and salt into a bowl and rub in the lard and butter until the mixture resembles breadcrumbs.

2 Add a little ice-cold water to form a dough.

3 On a floured board, roll out the dough as thinly as possible. Using a 3 cm/1¼ inch round pastry cutter, cut out circles and press into 12 half-size tartlet tins (mini tins). Prick the bottom of each tartlet case.

4 Place in a preheated oven and bake blind (unfilled) for approximately 6 minutes. Do not allow the pastry to brown. Gently remove from the tins, set on a cooling rack and leave to cool completely.

5 In the bottom of each tartlet case, spoon a little soured (sour) cream. Set 2 halves of a quail egg on end in the cream. Spoon a little caviar between the halves of egg and garnish with a sprig of dill.

Cured Beef and Baby Corn Canapés

METRIC/IMPERIAL	AMERICAN
350 g/12 oz lean beef fillet	¾ lb fillet of beef
50 ml/2 fl oz whisky	¼ cup Scotch whisky
2 garlic cloves, peeled	2 garlic cloves, peeled
2 sprigs thyme	2 sprigs thyme
2 sprigs rosemary	2 sprigs rosemary
2 bay leaves	2 bay leaves
1 stick celery, chopped	1 stick celery, chopped
½ onion, chopped	½ onion, chopped
1 chilli, seeded and sliced	1 hot chili pepper, seeded and sliced
2 dessertspoons rock salt	2 heaped teaspoons coarse Kosher salt
12 black peppercorns, crushed	12 black peppercorns, crushed
12 ears baby corn	12 ears baby corn

Serves 12

Preparation time: 10 minutes

Marinating and curing time: 8 days

1 In order to keep the fillet in shape, wrap it very tightly in a piece of muslin approximately 30 cm/12 inches square and tie securely with white thread.

2 Mix all the remaining ingredients, except the baby corn ears, together.

3 Place the beef in a large glass or earthenware bowl and pour the marinade over the top. Cover with cling film (saran wrap) and refrigerate for 5 days, turning the beef in the marinade every day.

4 Remove the beef, still in the muslin wrap, from the marinade and hang in a cold place to dry out for 3 days.

5 Unwrap the muslin and slice the beef as thinly as possible.

6 Wrap a slice of cured beef around an ear of baby corn. Lightly grill until warm and serve immediately.

Chicken Liver and Herb Pâté on a Bed of Spinach

*Spaghetti with Aubergines (Eggplant), Chilli, Garlic,
    Tomato and Mushrooms*

Almond Tarts with Brandy Sauce

Chicken Liver and Herb Pâté on a Bed of Spinach

METRIC/IMPERIAL	AMERICAN
175 g/6 oz raw chicken livers, trimmed	*¾ cup raw chicken livers, trimmed*
75 g/3 oz pork fat	*⅓ cup pork fat*
6 rashers streaky bacon	*6 strips lean bacon*
1 small apple, peeled, cored and chopped	*1 small apple, peeled, cored and chopped*
75 g/3 oz raw lean pork, trimmed	*3 oz raw lean pork, trimmed*
1 egg, size 4, beaten	*1 small egg, beaten*
1 x 5 ml spoon/1 teaspoon mixed herbs	*1 teaspoon mixed herbs*
1 small onion, peeled and chopped	*1 small onion, peeled and chopped*
250 ml/8 fl oz double cream	*1 cup heavy cream*
salt and pepper	*salt and pepper*

To serve

METRIC/IMPERIAL	AMERICAN
30 ml/½ tablespoon walnut oil	*1½ tablespoons walnut oil*
24 large spinach leaves, washed and dried	*24 large spinach leaves, washed and dried*
2 large ripe tomatoes, peeled, cored, seeded and cut into thin strips	*2 large ripe tomatoes, peeled, cored, seeded and cut into thin strips*

Serves 4

**Preparation time:
15-20 minutes**

**Chilling time:
1 hour**

**Cooking time:
1-1½ hours**

**Oven: 190°C, 375°F,
Gas Mark 5**

1 Finely mince (grind) together the chicken livers, pork fat, 2 rashers (strips) of bacon, apple and pork. Chill in the refrigerator for 1 hour.

2 Add the egg, herbs and onion and mix well in a bowl standing in a larger bowl of crushed ice. Add the cream a little at a time, beating vigorously, until well mixed. Add seasoning.

3 Line the base and sides of a 750 g/1½ lb terrine with the remaining bacon. Spoon the pâté mixture into the terrine, pressing down firmly so no air bubbles remain. The mixture should fill the terrine to within 2 cm/¾ inch of the top.

4 Cover the terrine with foil and a lid, set in a roasting tin half filled with hot water and cook in preheated oven for about 1 hour. To check if fully cooked, remove from the oven and push a roasting fork deep into the centre of the pâté. If the fork comes out clean, the pâté is cooked. If any of the mixture clings to the fork, return it to the oven and cook for a further 15-30 minutes. Leave to cool. Turn out the terrine and cut into slices, each approximately 2 cm/¾ inch thick.

5 Sprinkle the spinach leaves with the walnut oil and season with salt and pepper. Put 6 leaves on each plate, lay a slice of pâté on top, and arrange strips of tomato around the pâté.

Spaghetti with Aubergines (Eggplant), Chilli, Garlic, Tomato and Mushrooms

METRIC/IMPERIAL	AMERICAN
1.2 litres/2 pints water	2½ pints (5 cups) water
15 ml/½ fl oz cooking oil	1 tablespoon cooking oil
salt and pepper	salt and pepper
350 g/12 oz spaghetti	¾ lb spaghetti
25 g/1 oz butter	½ tablespoon butter
½ medium onion, finely chopped	½ medium onion, finely chopped
1 medium courgette, peeled and diced	1 medium zucchini, peeled and diced
1 small green pepper, cored, seeded and diced	1 small green pepper, cored, seeded and diced
1 small red pepper, cored, seeded and diced	1 small red pepper, cored, seeded and diced
1 small aubergine, diced	1 small eggplant, diced
1 Kenyan chilli, seeded, cored, rinsed and finely chopped	1 jalapeno or serrano chili, seeded, cored, rinsed and finely chopped
1 small garlic clove, peeled and chopped	1 small garlic clove, peeled and chopped
4 large open mushrooms, finely diced	4 large open mushrooms, finely diced
1 x 5 ml spoon/1 rounded teaspoon tomato purée	1 rounded teaspoon tomato purée
4 beef tomatoes, cut into 5mm/¼ inch dice	4 beefsteak tomatoes, cut into ¼ inch dice
8 fresh basil leaves, 2 chopped and 6 for garnish	8 fresh basil leaves, 2 chopped and 6 for garnish

Serves 4

Preparation time: 25 minutes

Cooking time: about 15 minutes

1 Pour the water into a large pan, add the oil and salt and bring to the boil.

2 Break the spaghetti into approximately 13 cm/5 inch lengths and cook until just tender. Drain well.

3 While the spaghetti is cooking, melt the butter in a heavy-based pan, add the chopped onion and cook, without colouring, for 3-4 minutes.

4 Add the courgettes (zucchini), peppers, aubergines (eggplants), chillis and garlic and cook gently, stirring continuously, for a further 5 minutes.

5 Add the mushrooms, tomato purée, tomatoes and the chopped basil and cook for a further 3 minutes. (The moisture from the vegetables will form the sauce.) Add seasoning to taste.

6 Place the spaghetti in individual bowls, top each with 3 dessertspoons (2 rounded tablespoons) of the vegetable mixture and garnish with a basil leaf.

Almond Tarts with Brandy Sauce

METRIC/IMPERIAL	AMERICAN
225 g/8 oz Sweet pastry (page 122)	8 oz Sweet pastry (page 122)

Filling	
4 dessertspoons raspberry jam	3 level tablespoons raspberry jam
40 g/1½ oz butter	3 tablespoons butter
40 g/1½ oz caster sugar	3 tablespoons superfine sugar
10 g/¼ oz plain flour	1 teaspoon all-purpose flour
50 g/2 oz ground almonds	⅔ cup ground almonds
1 egg, size 3, beaten	1 medium egg, beaten
15 g/½ oz flaked almonds	1 tablespoon flaked almonds

Brandy sauce	
2 egg yolks, size 3, beaten	2 medium egg yolks, beaten
20 g/¾ oz caster sugar	1½ tablespoons superfine or granulated sugar
drop of vanilla essence	drop of vanilla extract
175 ml/6 fl oz warm milk, boiled and strained	¾ cup warm milk, boiled and strained
45 ml/3 tablespoons brandy	3 tablespoons brandy

Almond Tart with Brandy Sauce

To decorate	12 fresh berries (blackberries, if possible)	*12 fresh berries* *(blackberries, if possible)*

Makes 4 individual tarts

Preparation time: 25 minutes

Cooking time: 20-25 minutes

Oven: 200°C, 400°F, Gas Mark 6

1 Grease four 10 cm/4 inch diameter tartlet cases.

2 On a lightly floured board, roll out the pastry, cut out 4 rounds and use to line the base and sides of the tins.

3 Put 1 dessertspoon (1 very heaped teaspoon) of raspberry jam in the bottom of each pastry case.

4 To make the filling, beat the butter and sugar together until light and fluffy. Add the flour, ground almonds and beaten egg.

5 Divide the mixture between the 4 tartlet tins and sprinkle with the flaked almonds.

6 Place in a preheated oven and bake for 20-25 minutes. Remove and leave to cool.

7 To make the brandy sauce, mix together the egg yolks, sugar and vanilla essence (extract). Whisk in the warm milk and pour the mixture into a heavy-based pan.

8 Cook over a low heat, stirring continuously with a wooden spoon, until the mixture coats the back of the spoon. Do not let it boil. Remove from the heat and leave to cool, then stir in the brandy.

9 For each serving, pour about 85 ml/2 fl oz/4 tablespoons of the sauce on one side of the plate. Cut the almond tart in half, slightly separating into 2 parts. Decorate with 3 berries set in a row on top of the sauce.

SCOTTISH BREAKFAST

Porage   *Oatcakes*

Loch Fyne Kippers

Cloutie Dumplings

Porage

METRIC/IMPERIAL	AMERICAN
600 ml/1 pint cold water	*1¼ pints cold water*
25 g/1 oz butter	*2 tablespoons butter*
1 x 5 ml spoon/1 teaspoon salt	*1 teaspoon salt*
50 g/2 oz oatmeal	*¾ cup Scotch oatmeal**
120 ml/4 fl oz double cream	*½ cup heavy cream*
10 g/¼ oz oatmeal, toasted	*2 tablespoons oatmeal, toasted*

*Scotch oatmeal is available in American speciality food shops and gourmet delicatessens. Do not use quick-cooking oatmeal.

Serves 4

Preparation time: 2 minutes

Cooking time: 20-25 minutes

1 Place the water, butter and salt in a pan and bring to the boil.
2 Reduce the heat, whisk in the oatmeal and cook gently for about 20 minutes until all the water is absorbed and the oatmeal is cooked.
3 Pour the porage into individual bowls and pour 25 ml/1 fl oz/2 tablespoons of cream over the top of each. Sprinkle each serving with a little toasted oatmeal.

Oatcakes

METRIC/IMPERIAL	AMERICAN
225 g/8 oz pinhead oatmeal*, plus extra for dusting	*3 cups pinhead oatmeal*, plus extra for dusting*
1½ x 5 ml spoons/1½ teaspoons caster sugar	*1½ teaspoons superfine or granulated sugar*
1 x 2.5 ml spoon/½ teaspoon baking powder	*½ teaspoon baking powder*
½ x 15 ml spoon/½ tablespoon plain flour	*½ tablespoon all-purpose flour*
1 x 5 ml spoon/1 teaspoon salt	*1 teaspoon salt*
50 g/2 oz butter, melted	*4 tablespoons butter, melted*
warm water, for mixing	*warm water, for mixing*

*Pinhead Scotch oatmeal is available in good grocery stores; if unobtainable, use best quality ground oats (oat groats) or porridge (rolled) oats.

Makes 24

Preparation time: 10 minutes

Cooking time: 15 minutes

Oven: 160°C, 325°F, Gas Mark 3

1 Mix the oatmeal, sugar, baking powder, flour and salt together.
2 Add the melted butter and mix thoroughly.
3 Add sufficient warm water to form a dough.
4 Dust a pastry board with oatmeal and roll out the dough to a thickness of 3 mm/⅛ inch. Using a 4 cm/1½ inch round cutter, cut out circles and place on a lightly greased baking (cookie) sheet.
5 Place in a preheated oven and bake for about 15 minutes. Cool on a rack, and store in an airtight tin.

Porage   Loch Fyne Kippers

Loch Fyne Kippers

METRIC/IMPERIAL

4 x 200g/7 oz kippers

melted butter

AMERICAN

*4 oak-smoked Scotch kippers,
each weighing ½ lb*
melted butter

Serves 4

**Preparation time:
2 minutes**

1 Cut off the head and tail of the kippers.
2 Brush with melted butter and grill on each side for about 3 minutes, brushing again with butter when the kipper is turned over.
3 Lift out the backbone and serve immediately.

Cooking time: 5-7 minutes

111

Cloutie Dumplings

METRIC/IMPERIAL

AMERICAN

METRIC/IMPERIAL	AMERICAN
50 g/2 oz plain flour	½ cup all-purpose flour
½ level teaspoon bicarbonate of soda	½ teaspoon baking soda
50 g/2 oz soft breadcrumbs	1 cup soft breadcrumbs
50 g/2 oz shredded suet	½ cup shredded suet
50 g/2 oz Demerara sugar	scant ½ cup light brown sugar, loosely packed
50 g/2 oz currants	⅓ cup currants
50 g/2 oz sultanas	⅓ cup white seedless raisins
50 g/2 oz raisins	⅓ cup dark raisins
1 egg, size 3, beaten	1 medium egg, beaten
ale or milk, to mix	beer or milk, to mix
oil, for frying	oil, for frying

Serves 4-5

Preparation time: 10 minutes

Cooking time: 2-3 hours

1 Sift the flour and bicarbonate of soda (baking soda) together. Mix with the breadcrumbs, suet and sugar. Toss the fruit in the mixture until well-coated.

2 Add the egg and ale (beer) or milk and stir well until the mixture forms a dropping consistency.

3 Scald a clean muslin cloth and rub it over with flour. Place the cloth in a bowl and pour in the mixture. Gather up the cloth, smoothing out as many folds as possible, then tie the ends together, allowing room for expansion. (Alternatively, the dumpling can be steamed in a pudding basin covered in foil.)

4 Turn a plate upside down in a heavy-based pan and set the pudding on it. Steam for 2-3 hours, topping up the water as required.

5 Remove the cloth carefully, to avoid breaking the skin of the pudding. Leave to cool completely.

6 When cold, cut into slices and shallow-fry in hot oil on both sides for the perfect accompaniment to a cooked breakfast – bacon, egg, sausages, grilled mushrooms and tomatoes.

FIRESIDE TEA

Mince Pies

Gingerbread

Madeira Cake

Rich Fruit Cake

Toasted Fruit Bread

Mince Pies

	METRIC/IMPERIAL	AMERICAN
Mincemeat	50 g/2 oz chopped suet	*½ cup chopped suet*
	50 g/2 oz mixed peel	*½ cup chopped candied peel*
	50 g/2 oz currants	*½ cup currants*
	50 g/2 oz sultanas	*⅓ cup white raisins*
	50 g/2 oz raisins	*⅓ cup dark raisins*
	50 g/2 oz apples, peeled and chopped	*1 small apple, peeled and chopped*
	50 g/2 oz Demerara sugar	*2 tablespoons light brown sugar*
	2 x 15 ml spoons/ 2 tablespoons mixed spice	*½ tablespoon each ground cinnamon, mace, cloves, nutmeg and allspice*
	zest and juice of 1 lemon	*zest and juice of 1 lemon*
	zest and juice of 1 orange	*zest and juice of 1 orange*
	25 ml/1 fl oz rum	*2 tablespoons rum*
	25 ml/1 fl oz brandy	*2 tablespoons brandy*
	25 ml/1 fl oz sherry	*2 tablespoons sherry*
Pastry	225 g/8 oz flour	*1½ cups all-purpose flour*
	150 g/5 oz butter	*10 tablespoons butter*
	50 g/2 oz caster sugar	*4 tablespoons superfine or granulated sugar*
	1 egg, size 1, beaten	*1 jumbo egg, beaten*
	milk, for brushing	*milk, for brushing*
	caster sugar, for sprinkling	*superfine sugar, for sprinkling*

Makes 10

**Preparation time:
15 minutes**

**Resting time:
3 days**

**Cooking time:
15 minutes**

**Oven: 230°C, 450°F,
Gas Mark 8**

1 To prepare the mincemeat, mix all the ingredients together in a bowl, cover and store in a cool place for about 3 days.

2 To make the pastry, rub or cut together the flour, butter and sugar. Add the egg and mix to form a firm but not crumbly dough. If the mixture is a little dry, add a few drops of ice-cold water.

3 Roll out the dough on a lightly floured board, and, using a 7.5 cm/3 inch pastry cutter, cut out 10 rounds for the pie bases. With a 6 cm/2½ inch pastry cutter, cut out 10 more rounds for the lids.

4 Line 10 sections of a tartlet tin with the pastry bases and place 1 dessertspoon/ 1 heaped teaspoon of mincemeat in each. (If there is any mincemeat left after the 10 cases are filled, add a little more to each.) Moisten the edges of the pastry cases and place the lids on top, pressing and crimping the edges together.

5 Brush the tops with milk and bake in a preheated oven for 15 minutes. Remove from the oven, slide off on to a rack, sprinkle with caster sugar and leave to cool.

Gingerbread

METRIC/IMPERIAL	AMERICAN
75 g/3 oz Demerara sugar	6 tablespoons light brown sugar
100 g/4 oz butter	4 oz butter
2 x 15 ml spoons/2 tablespoons black treacle	2 tablespoons dark molasses
2 eggs, size 1, beaten	2 jumbo eggs, beaten
4 x 15 ml spoons/4 tablespoons milk	4 tablespoons milk
300 g/11 oz plain flour	2 cups all-purpose flour
1 x 2.5 ml spoon/½ teaspoon bicarbonate of soda	½ teaspoon baking soda
1 x 2.5 ml spoon/½ teaspoon baking powder	½ teaspoon baking powder
50 g/2 oz mixed peel	½ cup candied cut peel
2 x 5 ml spoons/2 teaspoons ground ginger	2 teaspoons ground ginger

Yields 12 slices

Preparation time: 10 minutes

Cooking time: 1 hour 45 minutes

Oven: 150°C, 300°F, Gas Mark 2

1 Mix the sugar, butter and treacle (molasses) in a heavy-based pan and heat until the sugar has dissolved.

2 Beat the eggs and milk together in a bowl large enough to contain comfortably the whole mixture.

3 Sift the dry ingredients together.

4 Thoroughly mix the treacle (molasses) mixture into the eggs and milk, then beat in the dry ingredients to a smooth mixture.

5 Grease a 20 x 9 x 6 cm/8 x 3½ x 2½ inch loaf tin and line with greaseproof (waxed) paper. Pour the gingerbread mixture into the tin and bake in a preheated oven for about 1 hour 45 minutes. Turn out on to a rack, carefully peel off the paper and leave to cool.

Madeira Cake

METRIC/IMPERIAL	AMERICAN
225 g/8 oz butter	½ lb butter
225 g/8 oz sugar	1 heaped cup superfine or granulated sugar
4 eggs, size 1, beaten	4 jumbo eggs, beaten
225 g/8 oz flour	2 cups all-purpose flour
juice and zest of 1 orange	juice and zest of 1 orange
juice and zest of 1 lemon	juice and zest of 1 lemon

Yields 10-12 slices

Preparation time: 10 minutes

Cooking time: 1 hour 15 minutes

Oven: 160°C, 325°F, Gas Mark 3

1 Cream the butter and sugar until light and fluffy.

2 Add the beaten eggs a little at a time, mixing in a small quantity of flour if the mixture seems likely to curdle. Beat thoroughly.

3 Mix in the orange and lemon juice and zest, then fold in the flour, mixing gently but thoroughly.

4 Grease a 20 x 9 x 6 cm/8 x 3½ x 2½ inch loaf tin and transfer the mixture into the tin. Place in a preheated oven and bake for 1 hour 15 minutes. To test if it is fully cooked, insert a skewer in the centre of the cake – if it comes out clean, the cake is baked. Leave to cool slightly in the tin, then turn out on to a rack to cool completely before cutting.

In Braid's Cocktail Bar: Rich Fruit Cake   Toasted Fruit Bread
Gingerbread   Madeira Cake   Mince Pies

Rich Fruit Cake

METRIC/IMPERIAL	AMERICAN
150 g/5 oz butter	5 oz or 10 tablespoons butter
150 g/5 oz caster sugar	½ cup plus 2 tablespoons superfine or granulated sugar
3 eggs, size 1, beaten	3 jumbo eggs, beaten
225 g/8 oz plain flour	1½ cups all-purpose flour, unsifted
1 x 5 ml spoon/1 level teaspoon baking powder	1 level teaspoon baking powder
175 g/6 oz currants	1¼ cups currants
175 g/6 oz sultanas	1 cup white raisins
50 g/2 oz mixed peel	scant ½ cup candied fruit peel
grated rind of 1 lemon	grated rind of 1 lemon

Makes an 18cm/ 7 inch cake

Preparation time: 10 minutes

Cooking time: 2-2½ hours

Oven: 160°C, 325°F, Gas Mark 3

1 Cream the butter and sugar until light and fluffy.
2 Add the eggs a little at a time, mixing in a small amount of flour if the mixture looks as though it might curdle. Beat thoroughly.
3 Sift the flour with the baking powder and stir it into the mixture. Add the fruit, mixed peel (candied fruit peel) and lemon rind and stir well.
4 Line an 18 cm/7 inch round cake tin (bottom and sides) with greased grease-proof paper, and spoon the mixture into the tin, making a small depression in the top in the centre.
5 Place in a preheated oven and bake for 2-2½ hours. For the last hour of baking, cover the top of the cake with brown paper, to prevent overbrowning. To test if fully cooked, insert a skewer into the centre of the cake – if it comes out clean, the cake is baked. Leave in the tin for 15 minutes, then turn out on to a rack and peel the paper off the cake. Leave to cool before cutting.

Toasted Fruit Bread

METRIC/IMPERIAL	AMERICAN
350 g/12 oz self-raising flour	3 cups self-raising flour
50 g/2 oz caster sugar	4 tablespoons superfine or granulated sugar
2 x 5 ml spoons/2 teaspoons baking powder	2 teaspoons baking powder
50 g/2 oz dates, sliced	⅓ cup dates, sliced
25 g/1 oz raisins	2 tablespoons raisins
1 x 15 ml spoon/1 tablespoon golden syrup	1 tablespoon light corn syrup
1 x 15 ml spoon/1 tablespoon treacle	1 tablespoon molasses
300 ml/½ pint milk	1¼ cups milk

Makes 1 x 450 g/ 1 lb loaf

Preparation time: 15 minutes

Cooking time: 45-50 minutes

Oven: 180°C, 350°F, Gas Mark 4

1 Sift the flour, sugar and baking powder together. Add the dates and raisins.
2 Warm the golden (corn) syrup and treacle in a small pan and mix with the milk. Add this mixture to the dry ingredients and mix to a dropping consistency.
3 Grease a 450 g/1 lb loaf tin. Pour in the cake mixture and bake in a preheated oven for 45 – 50 minutes.
4 When a skewer pushed into the centre comes out clean, the loaf is cooked. Turn out on to a rack and leave to cool completely.
5 To serve, slice the loaf and butter each slice.

BASIC RECIPES

Brown (Beef, Veal, Duck) or Chicken Stock

METRIC/IMPERIAL	AMERICAN
1 kg/2 lb raw bones (beef, veal, game or chicken)	2 lb raw bones (beef, veal, game or chicken)
225 g/8 oz vegetables (carrots, onions, celery, leeks)	½ lb vegetables (carrots, onions, celery, leeks)
bouquet garni (thyme, bay leaf, parsley stalks)	bouquet garni (thyme, bay leaf, parsley stalks)
6 black peppercorns	6 black peppercorns
2 level dessertspoons salt	4 teaspoons salt

Makes 1.75 litres/ 3 pints/ 4 pints (US)

Cooking time: 8-9 hours

Oven: 220°C, 425° F, Gas Mark 7

1 Chop the bones and brown well on all sides by one of 2 methods: a) place in a roasting tin in a preheated oven for 45 minutes, or b) brown carefully for 10 minutes in a little fat in a frying pan.

2 Drain off any fat and put the bones in a stock pot. Set the roasting tin or frying pan over high heat, and brown the remaining sediment, scraping it from the bottom of the pan with a wooden spoon. Pour in 300 ml/½ pint/1¼ cups of water and simmer for a few minutes, then add to the bones. Do not discard the water. Add 2.25 litres/4 pints/5 pints (US) water. Bring to the boil and skim well.

3 Wash, peel and roughly chop the vegetables and gently fry in a little hot oil or fat until brown. Strain off the fat and add the vegetables to the stock pot. Add the bouquet garni, peppercorns and salt and simmer for 6-8 hours (2 hours for chicken stock). Skim off any froth that rises to the top from time to time. At the end of the cooking time, skim again thoroughly, strain and cool. This stock will keep 3-4 days in a refrigerator, or 2 months if frozen.

Fish Stock

METRIC/IMPERIAL	AMERICAN
25 g/1 oz butter or margarine	2 tablespoons butter or margarine
100 g/4 oz onions, peeled and sliced	1 medium onion, peeled and sliced
1 kg/2 lb white fish bones (preferably sole, whiting, turbot, etc), viscera and gills removed	2 lb white fish bones from any non-oily fish (flounder, sole, whiting, weakfish), viscera and gills removed
1 bay leaf	1 bay leaf
juice of ½ small lemon	juice of ½ a small lemon
parsley stalks	parsley stalks
3 peppercorns	3 peppercorns
2.25 litres/4 pints water	5 pints water

Makes 1.75 litres/ 3 pints/3¾ pints (US)

Preparation time: 10 minutes

Cooking time: 30 minutes

1 Melt the butter or margarine in a very large heavy-based pan. Add the onions, fish bones and all the other ingredients except the water. Cover the pan with greaseproof (waxed) paper and a lid and cook gently for 5 minutes.

2 Remove the paper and add the water. Bring to the boil, skim and simmer for 20 minutes only. Strain and cool.

3 Chill in the refrigerator, where it will keep for 2-3 days. Fish stock can be frozen for up to 1 month.

Beef Glaze

METRIC/IMPERIAL

1.2 litres/2 pints Beef stock
(page 117)
1 small onion, chopped
2 large mushrooms, washed and
roughly chopped
few parsley stalks
85 ml/3 fl oz dry red wine

AMERICAN

2½ pints Beef stock
(page 117)
1 small onion, chopped
2 large mushrooms, washed and
roughly chopped
few parsley stalks
⅓ cup dry red wine

Makes about 475 ml/
16-17 fl oz/1 pint (US)

1 Pour the beef stock into a large, heavy-based pan, set over a medium heat and reduce to one-quarter of its original volume: 300ml/½ pint/1¼ cups.
2 Add the chopped onions, mushrooms, parsley and wine and bring to the boil. Reduce the heat to a strong simmer and again reduce the volume by one-third.

Veal Glaze

METRIC/IMPERIAL

2.25 litres/2 pints Veal stock
(page 117)
½ onion, peeled and chopped
6 mushrooms, roughly chopped
few parsley stalks
150 ml/¼ pint dry red wine

AMERICAN

2½ pints Veal stock
(page 117)
½ onion, peeled and chopped
6 mushrooms, roughly chopped
few parsley stalks
generous ½ cup (5 fl oz) dry red
wine

Makes about 475 ml/
16-17 fl oz/1 pint (US)

1 Pour the stock into a heavy-based pan, bring to the boil and reduce to 600 ml/1 pint/1¼ pints.
2 Add the onion, mushrooms, parsley and wine and reduce by one-third.

Preparation time: 5 minutes   Cooking time: about 2 hours

Clarified Butter

Makes 500 g/1¼ lb/
20 oz

1 Melt 1 kg/2 lb/32 oz salted butter in a small pan and cook over a gentle heat, without stirring, until the butter begins to foam. Continue to cook the butter without browning until the foaming stops.
2 Remove the pan from the heat and let it stand until the milky deposits have sunk to the bottom, leaving a clear yellow liquid.
3 Pour this liquid carefully through a double layer of muslin wrung out in warm water into a bowl.
Clarified butter can be stored in a refrigerator for up to 6 weeks and can be used in liquid or solid form.

Béarnaise Sauce

METRIC/IMPERIAL	AMERICAN
2 shallots, chopped	*2 shallots, chopped*
2 x 15 ml spoons/2 tablespoons tarragon vinegar	*2 tablespoons tarragon vinegar*
15 g/½ oz chopped tarragon leaves	*1½ teaspoons chopped tarragon leaves*
10 peppercorns, crushed	*10 peppercorns, crushed*
4 egg yolks, size 1, beaten	*4 jumbo egg yolks, beaten*
350 g/12 oz Clarified butter, melted and cooled to tepid (opposite)	*1½ cups Clarified butter, melted and cooled to tepid (opposite)*
1 dessertspoon chopped parsley	*1 rounded teaspoon chopped parsley*

Makes generous 450 ml/15 fl oz/ scant pint (US)

Preparation time: 5 minutes

1 Place the shallots, vinegar, tarragon, and peppercorns in a heavy-based pan. Bring to the boil and reduce by half. Leave to cool.
2 Add the egg yolks and whisk over a bowl of hot water until light and fluffy. Remove from the heat and gradually add the melted butter, whisking all the time. If the sauce becomes too thick, add a little hot water.
3 Strain into a clean bowl and add the parsley. Serve the sauce warm.

Cooking time: approximately 8-10 minutes

Tomato Coulis

METRIC/IMPERIAL	AMERICAN
25 g/1 oz butter	*2 tablespoons butter*
¼ medium onion, chopped	*1 small onion, chopped*
3 basil leaves, chopped	*3 basil leaves, chopped*
10 tomatoes, roughly chopped	*10 tomatoes, roughly chopped*
few drops of Tabasco	*few drops of Tabasco*
1 x 2.5 ml spoon/½ teaspoon Worcestershire sauce	*½ teaspoon Worcestershire sauce*
salt and pepper	*salt and pepper*

Makes 600 ml/ 1 pint/1¼ pints (US)

1 Melt the butter in a pan, add the onion and chopped basil and cook gently for a few minutes.
2 Add the tomatoes, cover the pan and cook for about 15 minutes until very soft.
3 Pour the mixture into a liquidizer, add the sauces and blend well. Season.
4 Strain the sauce through a fine sieve to remove all skin and seeds. Leave to cool.

Wild Rice

METRIC/IMPERIAL	AMERICAN
150 g/5 oz wild rice	*¾ cup wild rice*
600 ml/1 pint water	*2½ cups water*
15 g/½ oz butter or margarine (optional)	*1 tablespoon butter or margarine (optional)*
salt and pepper	*salt and pepper*

Wild rice is not real rice, but a 'water grain', often called 'The Caviar of Grains'. It grows along the margins of lakes in the Northern United States, and traditionally is harvested by hand by local Indian tribes. It is especially delicious with game birds, chicken or turkey or grilled fish.

1 Wash the wild rice in several changes of cold water. Bring the water and butter (if using) to the boil. Add the rice and seasoning and stir.
2 Cover and simmer gently for about 55 minutes until the rice is tender and all the water is absorbed. Drain thoroughly.

Pommes Rosti

METRIC/IMPERIAL	AMERICAN
4 large potatoes	*4 large potatoes*
salt and pepper	*salt and pepper*
20 g/¾ oz butter	*scant 2 tablespoons butter*
40 ml/1½ fl oz (3 tablespoons) cooking oil	*3 tablespoons cooking oil*

Serves 4

Preparation time:
5 minutes

Cooking time:
about 35 minutes

Oven: 200°C, 400°F,
Gas Mark 6

1 Wash and peel the potatoes and coarsely grate into a bowl. Press hard through a sieve, then wring out in a dry tea towel, to remove excess moisture. (Wash the towel immediately as the potato juice will stain.) Season with salt and pepper.
2 Melt the butter with the oil in an ovenproof frying pan and heat until the mixture starts to smoke. Pour the grated potatoes into the pan, emptying the bowl away from you, to avoid being splashed with hot oil.
3 Press the mixture down with a palette knife (wide spatula), to ensure an even thickness across the pan. The mixture should resemble a thick pancake. Cook until the underside forms a golden-brown crust.
4 Using a palette knife or fish slice (pancake turner), carefully remove the rosti from the pan. (Alternatively, place an inverted plate over the pan and slide the potatoes out). Add a little more oil to the pan and heat until hot, tilting the pan to coat the bottom and sides of the pan thoroughly. Return the potato mixture to the pan, cooked-side up.)
5 Place in a preheated oven and cook for about 15 minutes until the potatoes are cooked through.
6 Turn the rosti out on to a baking tin or plate and leave to cool slightly. Cut into 4 rounds, using a 7.5 cm/3 inch diameter cutter.

Sauce Anglaise

METRIC/IMPERIAL	AMERICAN
150 ml/5 fl oz milk	*½ cup plus 4 tablespoons milk*
75 ml/2½ fl oz double cream	*5 tablespoons heavy cream*
zest of ½ small lemon	*zest of ½ small lemon*
zest of ½ small orange	*zest of ½ small orange*
3 egg yolks, size 2	*3 large egg yolks*
50 g/2 oz caster sugar	*4 tablespoons superfine or granulated sugar*

Makes 400 ml/
scant 15 fl oz/
scant pint (US)

Preparation time:
5 minutes

Cooking time:
15 minutes

1 Mix the milk, cream, lemon and orange zest and half the sugar in a heavy-based pan and bring gently to simmering point.
2 Whisk the egg yolks and remaining sugar together until light and fluffy. Pour the hot milk mixture gradually on to the egg and sugar, beating constantly.
3 Place the pan over a high heat and bring just to simmering point, stirring constantly and reaching all around the pan with the spoon. The sauce must not boil. Heat until the mixture coats the back of a metal spoon. If it is too thin, lower the heat and simmer gently to a coating consistency.
4 Strain into a bowl and leave to cool. The sauce will keep for 3 days in the refrigerator, with a sheet of cling film pressed on to the surface and the bowl tightly covered with extra cling film (saran wrap).

Stock Syrup

METRIC/IMPERIAL	AMERICAN
225 g/8 oz caster sugar	1 cup superfine or granulated sugar
300 ml/½ pint water	1¼ cups water
juice of 1 lemon	juice of 1 lemon
juice of 1 orange	juice of 1 orange

Makes 450 ml/
¾ pint/
scant pint
(15 fl oz) (US)

1 Combine all the ingredients in a saucepan and boil until all the sugar has completely dissolved.
2 Strain and leave to cool. Store in a tightly stoppered bottle in the refrigerator.

Preparation time: 20 minutes

Ginger Coulis

METRIC/IMPERIAL	AMERICAN
200 ml/⅓ pint Stock syrup (above)	⅞ cup (7 fl oz) Stock syrup (above)
15 g/1 tablespoon ground ginger	1 tablespoon powdered ginger
15 g/1 tablespoon powdered gelatine	1 tablespoon gelatin powder

Makes 200 ml/
⅓ pint/7 fl oz

1 Mix the stock syrup and ground ginger in a small pan and bring to the boil.
2 Dissolve the gelatine in the hot mixture. Remove from the heat, strain and leave to cool.

Raspberry Coulis

METRIC/IMPERIAL	AMERICAN
50 ml/ 2 fl oz water	¼ cup water
450 g/1 lb fresh or frozen raspberries	1 lb fresh or frozen raspberries
75 g/3 oz caster sugar	6 tablespoons (⅜ cup) superfine or granulated sugar

Makes 300 ml/
½ pint/1¼ cups

Preparation time:
30 minutes

1 Bring the water to the boil in a heavy-based pan, add the raspberries and sugar and simmer until very soft.
2 Press the mixture through a conical strainer, transfer to a jam (jelly) bag and leave suspended over a basin until all the juice has drained through. The bag must be supported so that the bottom of it does not dip into the juice in the basin.
3 Pour the clear juice into a small bowl, cover and refrigerate until ready to serve.

Puff Pastry

AMERICAN

225 g/8 oz plain flour   *½ lb (1½ cups) all-purpose flour*
salt   *salt*
225 g/8 oz margarine or   *½ lb margarine or butter,*
butter, very cold   *very cold*
150 ml/¼ pint ice-cold water   *generous ½ cup (5 fl oz) ice-cold*
                                                water
few drops of lemon juice   *few drops of lemon juice*

Note: care must be taken when rolling out the paste to keep the ends and sides square. The lightness of the paste is caused by the air which is trapped when folding the pastry during preparation.

Makes 500 g/ 1¼ lb

Preparation time: 20 minutes

Resting time: 1 hour 50 minutes

1 Sift the flour and salt into a bowl. Rub or cut in with a pastry blender, 50 g/2 oz/ 4 tablespoons of the fat.

2 Make a well in the centre and add the water and lemon juice. Knead well into a smooth dough to form a ball. Leave the dough to rest in a cool place for 30 minutes.

3 Cut a cross half way through the dough and pull out the corners to form a star shape. Roll out the points of the star square, leaving the centre thick.

4 Knead the remaining fat to the same texture as the dough. (This is most important: if the fat is too soft it will melt and ooze out, if too hard it will break through the paste when being rolled.)

5 Place the fat on the thick centre of the star shape and fold over the flaps. Roll out to approximately 30 x 15 cm/12 x 6 inches, cover with a cloth and leave to rest in a cool place for 20 minutes.

6 Roll out to approximately 60 x 20 cm/24 x 8 inches, fold both ends into the centre and fold in half again to form a square – this is one double turn. Leave to rest in a cool place for 20 minutes.

7 Half turn the paste to the right or left and roll out again. Give one more double turn (Step 6), roll out and leave to rest for 20 minutes. Give the pastry 2 more double turns, rolling out and resting between each turn. Leave to rest for another 20 minutes before using.

Sweet Pastry

AMERICAN

65 g/2½ oz butter   *2 oz plus 2 tablespoons butter*
25 g/1 oz caster sugar   *2 tablespoons superfine sugar*
½ egg, size 4, beaten   *1 very small egg, beaten*
100 g/4 oz flour   *1 cup all-purpose flour*

Makes 225 g/8 oz

1 Cream together the butter and sugar.

2 Add the egg gradually, then mix in the flour to form a dough.

3 Chill for 30 minutes before rolling out.

The following sorbets can be included in any of the menus as a refreshing interlude between the starter and the main course.

Apple Mint Sorbet

METRIC/IMPERIAL	AMERICAN
1 large sprig fresh apple mint	*1 large sprig fresh apple mint*
100 ml/3½ fl oz boiling water	*7 tablespoons boiling water*
250 ml/8 fl oz Stock	*1 cup Stock syrup*
syrup (page 121)	*(page 121)*
1 egg white, size 4, lightly	*1 small egg white, lightly*
beaten	*beaten*

Serves 4

Preparation time: about 8 minutes

Freezing time: about 30-35 minutes

1 Strip the apple mint leaves from their stem and infuse them in the boiling water for 5 minutes. Leave to cool.

2 Mix the liquid with the stock syrup and pour into a sorbet machine or ice-cream maker and freeze, following the manufacturers' instructions, for 15 – 20 minutes until it is slushy.

3 Add the egg white, mix thoroughly and continue to freeze until a sorbet consistency is reached.

4 Place the sorbet in a piping (pastry) bag fitted with a star nozzle and pipe into individual ramekin dishes.

VARIATION: LEMON THYME SORBET
Serves 4
Prepare as for Apple Mint Sorbet, but substitute 1 heaped teaspoonful of lemon thyme leaves, stripped from their stems.

Fresh Strawberry Sorbet

METRIC/IMPERIAL	AMERICAN
300 ml/½ pint Stock syrup	*1¼ cups Stock syrup*
(page 121)	*(page 121)*
75 ml/3 fl oz strawberry purée	*6 tablespoons strawberry purée*
1 egg white, size 3, lightly	*1 medium egg white, lightly*
beaten	*beaten*

Serves 4

Preparation time: 8-10 minutes

Freezing time: about 30 minutes

1 Mix together the stock syrup and strawberry purée. Place in a sorbet machine or ice-cream maker and freeze, following the manufacturers' instructions, for about 15 minutes or until slushy.

2 Add the egg white, mix thoroughly and continue to freeze until a sorbet consistency is reached.

3 Place the sorbet in a piping (pastry) bag fitted with a star nozzle and pipe into individual ramekin dishes. Alternatively, scoop the sorbet into a plastic container, cover and place in the freezer. Transfer the sorbet to the refrigerator about 20 minutes before serving.

Fondant Icing

METRIC/IMPERIAL	AMERICAN
225 g/8 oz granulated sugar	½ lb superfine or granulated sugar
120 ml/4 fl oz water	½ cup water
½ teaspoon liquid glucose or pinch of cream of tartar	pinch of cream of tartar

Makes 225 g/ 8 oz/½ lb

Preparation time: about 15 minutes

Cooking time: 10-15 minutes

1 In a small deep saucepan, stir the sugar into the water over a low heat. Do not allow it to boil.

2 In a saucer, stir the cream of tartar to a smooth consistency with about a teaspoonful of water. Add to the sugar syrup. Cover and bring to the boil – when you hear it begin to simmer remove the cover. Insert a sugar or deep- frying thermometer and boil the mixture to 115°C/240°F. If you do not have a thermometer, cook until a small spoonful dropped into a bowl of ice-cold water will form a soft ball when kneaded between the fingers. Remove from the heat and stand the pan in a deeper pan of cold water to cool slightly.

3 Run cold water over a cold smooth surface (ideally, marble). Pour on the fondant and with a palette knife (spatula), turn the outside edges towards the centre. Keep on turning it in on itself until it is moderately stiff, and begins to look grainy and opaque. Scrape it up into a ball and knead it with your hands until it is smooth and even.

4 To use within a few hours: place the fondant ball in a bowl and cover with a damp cloth.

5 To store: place in an airtight tin or a jar with a tight screw top. Before use, warm it in a bowl over hot water.

6 Fondant can be rolled out on a board covered lightly with icing (confectioners' powdered) sugar and cut into the desired shape.

Brandy Snap Baskets

METRIC/IMPERIAL	AMERICAN
45 g/1¾ oz caster sugar	3 tablespoons superfine or granulated sugar
50 g/2 oz butter	4 tablespoons butter
85 ml/3 fl oz maple syrup	6 tablespoons maple syrup
40 g/1½ oz flour	2½ tablespoons flour
5 g/⅛ oz ground ginger	¼ teaspoon ground ginger

Makes 4

Preparation time: 5 minutes

Cooling time: 30 minutes

Cooking time: 8-10 minutes

Oven: 180°C, 350°F, Gas Mark 4

1 Stir the sugar, butter and maple syrup together in a pan and heat until melted.

2 Sift the flour and ginger together. Add the melted butter mixture and mix well. Leave to cool for 30 minutes.

3 Drop 4 generously heaped teaspoons of the mixture on to a well-oiled baking (cookie) sheet, spacing well apart to allow for expansion. Bake in a preheated oven for 8-10 minutes until golden brown.

4 Remove from the oven and leave on the baking (cookie) sheet to cool for a minute or two, then while they are still pliable remove with a palette knife (spatula) and shape around 4 inverted cups. Leave until cool and crisp and remove carefully.

INDEX

Shrimp (Mediterranean prawns) with sweet chili sauce 58
Sliced banana and strawberries with honey ice cream and chocolate sauce 57
Sliced breast of baby chicken with lettuce and pecan nut salad 32
Sliced breast of guinea fowl with red currants 16
Sliced fresh fruit with melted chocolate 83
Smoked crab and chicory (endive) salad with chive mayonnaise 92
Smoked mackerel, baby herring and mussel salad with mustard and caviar dressing 44
Smoked salmon and slices of pear filled with cottage cheese and chives 74
Smoked salmon canapés 105
Sole:
   Trout mousse wrapped in sole with champagne cream sauce 21
Sorbet:
   Apple mint sorbet 58, 123
   Fresh strawberry sorbet 24, 123
   Mango sorbet 94
Soufflé:
   Chilled Grand Marnier soufflé 64
Soups:
   Carrot and orange soup 77
   Chilled fennel and cucumber soup with grated carrot 51
   Cream of asparagus soup with crushed toasted almonds 20
   Cream of chicken soup with sorrel and fine pasta 101
   Vegetable and leek broth 80
   Watercress soup with fresh thyme and cream 47
Spaghetti with aubergines (eggplant), chilli, garlic, tomato and mushrooms 108
Spiced cocktail sauce 70
Spinach and courgette (zucchini) sauce 57
Squab:
   Squab (pigeon) breast with walnut and orange vinaigrette 88
Stilton and red wine pâté 78
Stock syrup 19, 28, 95, 121
Stocks:
   Beef 28, 94, 117
   Chicken 20, 51, 117
   Duck 117
   Fish 39, 63, 71, 117
   Veal 18, 117
Strawberries:
   Fanned melon with fresh berries and apple mint yogurt 62
   Fresh strawberry sorbet 25, 123
   Leaf pastry with Drambuie cream and strawberries 48
   Sliced banana and strawberries with honey ice cream and chocolate sauce 57
Studded collops of beef with marinated grapes 92
Sugared bananas flamed in white rum 103

Sweet chilli sauce 58
Sweet pastry 41, 67, 122
Sweet peppers filled with fine vegetable mousse and fresh tomato sauce 55

Toasted fruit bread 116
Tomato coulis 37, 55, 72, 119
Tomatoes:
   Marinated vegetables in tomato shells 16
Trout mousse wrapped in sole with champagne cream sauce 21
Turbot:
   Broiled halibut and turbot steaks with sauces of rosemary and sorrel 38

Veal:
   Escalope of veal with braised Chinese cabbage 47
   Rolled loin of veal and lamb with crushed hazelnuts and apricot sauce 29
   Rolled veal and beef fillets with shallots and garlic 25
   Veal and ham pie 85
Veal and ham pie 85
Veal glaze 18, 30, 82, 118
Veal stock 18, 117
Vegetable and leek broth 80
Vegetable gâteau with tomato and basil purée 37
Vegetable kebab with wild rice and pepper sauce 33
Vegetables:
   Asparagus and artichoke quiches with spinach and courgette (zucchini) sauce 56
   Marinated vegetables in tomato shells 16
   Sweet peppers filled with fine vegetable mousse and fresh tomato sauce 55
Vegetables with soya (soy) sauce and saffron rice 99
Vegetables wrapped in filo pastry with a cream broccoli sauce 59
Venison pâté with blackcurrant sauce 79
Vinaigrette:
   Raspberry vinaigrette 53
   Walnut and orange vinaigrette 88

Walnut and orange vinaigrette 88
Watercress soup with fresh thyme and cream 47
Wholemeal loaves with ham and pineapple, cream cheese and grapes 79
Wholemeal toasted croûtons of smoked, marinated and creamed salmon 24
Wild rice 34, 39, 119